A RUMINATION

Carl Hileman

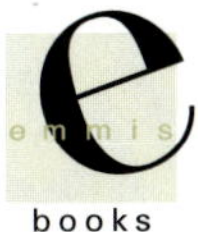

books

Permissions

THE PATIENCE OF COWS is an online quote attributed to Frank Lloyd Wright, source unknown./ THE HEROISM OF COWS is reprinted from The *Telegraph,* United Kingdom, February 18, 2004./"The Last Time Shorty Towers Fetched the Cows" by Wesley McNair was first published in *The Town of No,* by David Godine Books and is reprinted with permission of the poet./THE AFTERLIFE OF COWS, by Jack Sage, is printed by permission of his widow, Dawn Sage./"The Two-Headed Calf" by Laura Gilpin was first published in *The Hocus Pocus of the Universe* by Doubleday and is reprinted with permission of the poet./THE TEACHERSHIP OF COWS article on Jeff Byers is reprinted with the permission of Shirley Skeel and *California Coast & Ocean* magazine./STUBBORNNESS OF COWS is taken from *The Life of Ralph Waldo Emerson* by Richard Garnett, published by Kessinger Publishing./WANDERLUST OF COWS was taken in part from *D. H. Lawrence & Susan His Cow,* by William York Tindall, Columbia University Press; *The Later D. H. Lawrence,* by William York Tindall, published by Knopf; and *The Biography of D H Lawrence,* by John Worthen, published by the University of Nottingham./THE VANITY OF COWS is reprinted from as Associated Press story, February 5, 2004./THE GENETICS OF COWS is reprinted from *OpinionJournal.com,* May 21, 2002./"That Morning" was first printed in *Important Words, A Book for Poets and Writers,* Heinemann Press, and is used by permission of the poet, Bill Brown./THE ESCAPADE OF COWS is a first-person account by Flora Strong Farmer and is printed here by permission of her children—Frank Farmer, of Tampa, FL; Lois White of Albion, MI; and Betty Duvall, of Shreveport, LA./LOVE OF COWS was first published in *StarTribune.com,* February 5, 2001. It is reprinted here with permissio of Erica Johnson./THE MISAPPROPRIATION of COWS article is reprinted from News.com.au, Correspondents in London, February 20, 2004./"The New Cow," by August Derleth, was first published in *Here On A Darkling Plain,* by Ritten House of Philadelphia, 1940, and later collected in Derleth's anthology of poems, *Selected Poems,* circa 1944. It is reprinted by permission of his daughter and son, April Rose and Walde William Derleth./"So You Want to Milk a Cow" was first printed in *Wate Works Wonders, A History of the White, Wilson, McMahon, River Junction School Districts* and is reprinted by permission of the author, Helen Doenz./THE POLITICS OF COWS is reprinted from an interview with President George W. Bush, *Paris Match Magazine,* May 28, 2004./"Watching the Mil Cows,"by Sandra Adelmund, was first published in *Voices on the Prairie* by Loess Hills Books and is reprinted by permission of the poet. "Cows at Night" was first published by Nidus, and is used by permission of the poet, Charles Fishman.THE HISTORY OF COWS by W. M. Nagiller i an excerpt taken from *Trail Drivers of Texas,* which was first printed in 1925, by Cokesbury Press./THE DIVINITY OF COWS contains two quotes t are reprinted from a collection of lectures on the Srimad Bhagavatam, given by His Divine Grace A.C. Bhaktivedanta Swami Prabhupada, published by Bhaktivedanta Book Trust International, Inc./"Milk Don' Come from a Bottle," is printed by permission of Dave Prosser./"A Co Bow," is printed by permission of the author, Terry Kay.

For further information, contact the publisher at

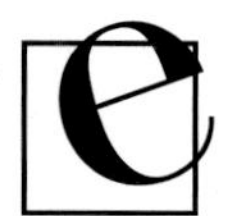

Emmis Books
1700 Madison Road
Cincinnati, Ohio 45206
www.emmisbooks.com

ISBN 1-57860-187-8
Library of Congress Control Number: 2004111194

Dedication

MARISSA SHAE GUENTHER, the special little four year-old who brightens my life beyond belief, and has been with me many times to explore the wonders of nature, including cows.

BRYAN HILEMAN, my son, who was a little "Jack O the Woods," traipsing miles with me through forests and fields when his legs weren't long enough to keep up. Thank you, Bryan, for sharing my life in that way.

DRAKE THOMAS HILEMAN, my first grandson, who will be born in the fall of 2004.

JIM HOUSEHOLDER, my friend, who passed away before the publication of this book. Jim always loved the art I made, and was an artist at heart himself.

Acknowledgments

I want to extend a heartfelt thanks to the following people who helped make this book possible, and journey so enjoyable:

Carl L. Hileman and **Margaret Ann Hileman**, my parents, for their life-long support.
And **Sharon Hesselmeyer**, for her unyielding belief in me.

The talented crew at **Emmis Books**, for all their hard work and dedication to this project:
Jack Heffron, editor; **Richard Hunt**, publisher; **Howard Cohen**, publicist; **Katie Parker**, sales director; **Meg Cannon**, marketing manager; **Andrea Kupper/Dana Boll**, designers; **Ann Comello**, business manager; **Mary Schuetz**,sales manager; and **Sarah Crabtree**, administrative assistant.

And to **Jeffrey Kleinman**, who co-agented this book with Cathie Pelletier.

Josh Sanseri, Lyle Fuchs, Ann Dodge, Dan Overturf, Heather Lose and **Scott Kemmerer**, for their technical assistance.
Tom Viorikic, for help and advice, and **Dave Prosser**, for writing "Milk Don't Come From a Bottle."

To all the **Artists** and **Writers** who generously shared their experiences with, and thoughts about, cows. I am greatly indebted.

Carroll and **Joyce Mowery**, **Mark** and **Lisa Glabb**, **Jerry Clutts**, and the many other farmers who so graciously allowed me into their pastures.

And to the **COWS**. Without them, the world would be a different place.

And last, but certainly not least, a special word of gratitude to **Cathie Pelletier**, my life-long friend, partner in many endeavors, and one of the most talented people I have ever known, for her total dedication and the endless hours of work she contributed to this book. Simple words can not express my appreciation. Thanks, Cat.

Table of Contents

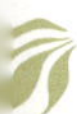

Introduction

I often worked on local farms as a teenager, pitching hay, building fences, or working with stock. One Saturday morning I got a call from Donald Wilkerson, a farmer I had known for a time and worked for on occasion. He needed help, and I was ready to make some spending money. When I got to Donny's farm, he was putting empty burlap feed sacks into the truck.

"What are those for?" I asked. He pointed to the middle of the pasture, to where a lone cow was lying on the ground.

"She's calving," Donny said. "And she's in trouble."

Being a country boy, I knew what he meant, but I didn't know the details. When we got to the cow, her calf was turned the wrong way. I had seen a calf born before but I had never been in this situation.

"What do we do?" I asked.

"We turn the calf inside her," Donny told me. "We help deliver it."

I was still wondering about the burlap sacks as the cow bawled up at us. She was in pain, and it seemed as if she were asking us to do something. Donny bent down and, to my amazement, he inserted both hands into her birth canal, began moving the calf around. Once he was convinced that the calf was in the right position, he told me to go get the burlap sacks. When I got back to Donny and the cow, she was having a contraction. I could see the little calf slowly beginning to show. In a few minutes, it had emerged about eight inches.

"Pick up a sack, Carl, and grab hold," Donny said. Now I knew what the burlap was for. It would stick to the membrane around the calf, allowing for a good grip. I did as Donny told me, pulling gently at first, thinking I might hurt the mother if I did it with any more force.

"You gotta pull harder!" Donny told me. So I put my back into it, and in a flash that tiny calf, water, and afterbirth all came flooding out. I was amazed. I just stood there for a moment gazing at this miracle of life. It was a cold autumn morning with frost on the ground, and the little spotted calf was steaming and shivering. "Blow in her nose," Donny said. And he smiled.

"What, are you kidding me?" I asked. He shook his head.

"Blow in her nose, and she'll never forget you."

So I bent down beside this steaming, wobbling little creature, held its head in my hands, and blew a breath into her nostrils. I felt good about what I'd been a part of that fall morning, knowing the mother and calf would most likely have died without our help.

I got paid that day, but I would have done it for nothing.

Thus began my interest in, and relationship with, those bovines who share the planet earth with us humans. In the summer of 1999, I began photographing cows for an exhibition. My purpose was to make people aware of how important the lowly cow really is, and how much we have integrated this animal into our

everyday lives. Along with historical and scientific information, I wanted the visual images to elevate the cow in a way that hadn't been done. This is the main reason that I used infrared film. I wanted to set the cows I photographed apart from the usual comic, even dumb portrayal that we often see. Most of the photographs in this book were shot while I was lying flat on my stomach, or at a low angle. I wanted to empower the cows, make them the Citizen Kanes of the animal world. I wanted *them* to tower over *us* for a change.

Infrared film is difficult and unpredictable because it demands some extra attention. It requires a special filtration and must be loaded and unloaded in total darkness, which presents problems in the field. This film records reflective infrared energy. Therefore, tree leaves, grass, or any vegetation will absorb more of these light waves than other objects, giving them a frost-covered appearance in photographs.

I shot this series of photographs on many different farms scattered throughout Southern Illinois. I sought out the ones belonging to small cattle farmers since I am opposed to large factory farms. These smaller operations gave me the opportunity to work more closely with the cows. Added to that, I was told personal stories about many of them by the farmers who owned them. This in turn often inspired me, even helped me determine how I might photograph the cow in question. It took a year for me to finish the series of photos you see in this book. But it's not over yet. I still find myself stopping my truck on some back country road, grabbing my camera, and walking over to the fence where a cow is peering curiously at me.

So then, what did I learn, all those mornings that I lay flat on my stomach in some farmer's field or barnyard, the smell of fresh cow pies wafting over to greet me? I went into the venture thinking I already knew a lot about cows. All that remained was getting the photographs. But I was wrong. What I learned is that I knew very little. Cows are individuals, their personalities as varied as they are with humans. They are extremely protective of their young. They can be gentle, and they can be harsh. While photographing them, I was urinated on and even charged. But I was also nuzzled many times, and my coat sleeve was licked lovingly.

When the opportunity arose to put my photographs into book form, along with text, I thought it would be a great vehicle to let others share their personal experiences and thoughts about cows. I have met very few people who don't have something to say about these unique animals. As this book came together, so did the folks who told me their own stories and adventures, from all corners of the United States, Canada, and even England. This is a collaborative effort, and I thank them all for taking the time to put words to my photos.

I don't know if Donny Wilkerson was right, that cold autumn morning almost forty years ago, when he told me that if I blew into the nostrils of the newborn calf it would never forget me. But I do know this: *I* have never forgotten that *calf*.

Carl Hileman
Tamms, Illinois

The Patience of Cows

Has anyone sung the song of the patient, calf-bearing,
milk-flowing, cud-chewing, tail-switching cow?

—Frank Lloyd Wright

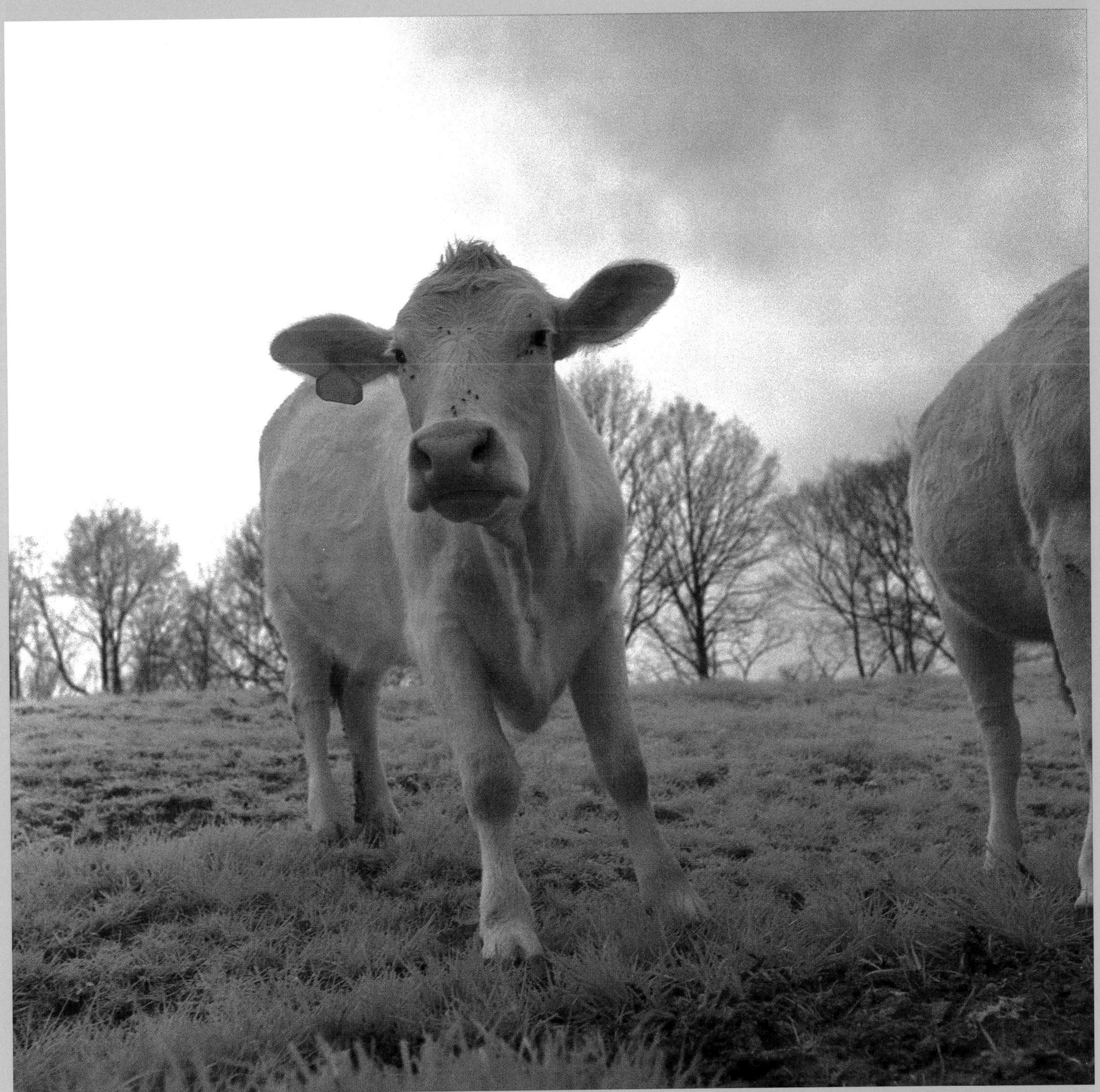

The Defamation of Cows

Late one night, when we were all in bed,
Mrs. O'Leary lit a lantern in the shed.
Her cow kicked it over,
Then winked her eye and said,
"There'll be a hot time in the old town tonight!"

—Joe Hayden, Popular Song Lyric, 1896

I could not tell anything of the fire only that two men came by the door. I guess it was my husband got outside the door and he ran back to the bedroom and said, "Kate, the barn is afire!" I ran out and the whole barn was on fire.

I was in bed myself and my husband and five children when this fire commenced. I was the owner of them five cows that was burnt, and the horse wagon and harness. I had two tons of coal and two tons of hay. I had everything that I wanted in for the winter. I could not save five cents worth of anything out of the barn. Only that Mr. Sullivan got out a little calf. The calf was worth eleven dollars on Saturday morning. Saturday morning I refused even eleven dollars for the calf, and it was sold afterwards for eight dollars.

I never had five cents insurance—I had those cows. One of them was not in the barn that night. It was out in the alley. That one went away. I could not get that one. My husband spent two weeks looking for it and could not find it anywhere in the world. I could not get five cents.

I had six cows there. A good horse there. I had a wagon and harness and everything I was worth. I couldn't save that much out of it (snapping her finger) and upon my word I worked so hard for them.

(*Court testimony of Kate O'Leary, whose cow was wrongly blamed for starting the Great Chicago Fire—October, 1871.*)

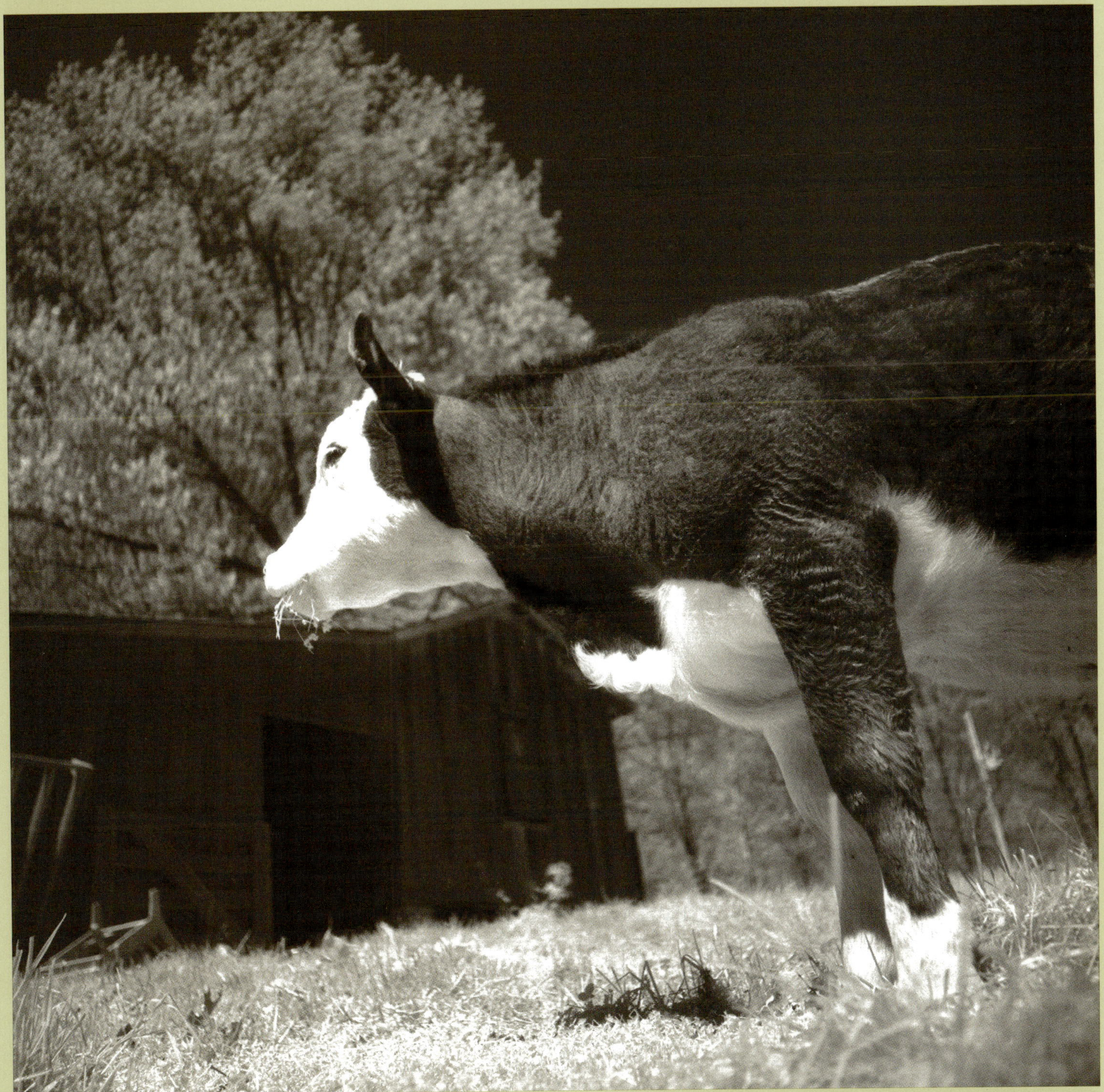

The Support of Cows

by Doug Kershaw

Some of the happiest memories I have from my childhood in the swamps of Southwest Louisiana were the days we spent on our houseboat, following the fish up and down the Mermentau River. When winter came we tied up permanently along the banks, and our lives took on a kind of routine.

By the time I was five years old, I had my own fiddle. This was one that my Uncle Abel had made for me out of an empty cigar box, sewing thread, and window screen wires. He hoped that by giving me the cigar-box fiddle it would keep my mind off the real fiddle that my father, Daddy Jack, kept up on a cabinet out of my reach. This plan of his worked for quite some time, too.

Back then, the family owned a horse and three friendly milk cows. These four were my first audience, and they didn't seem to mind that my fiddle wasn't real. The horse, however, soon lost interest and would go back to eating hay or just wander off. I couldn't seem to "hold" the horse.

But the cows, man, they loved listening to my fiddle! They'd chew their cuds, and sometimes tilt their heads, or swish their tails like they were applauding. I'd introduce each song to them, out of courtesy, and they seemed to appreciate that. When the tune finished, I always remembered to bow to them, too, to show them that I appreciated their support.

Thinking back, it's a damn good thing we had those cows, and not just horses. Horses would have given me an inferiority complex. But those friendly milk cows gave me the impression that maybe I could go off in the world one day and become an entertainer.

So that's what I did.

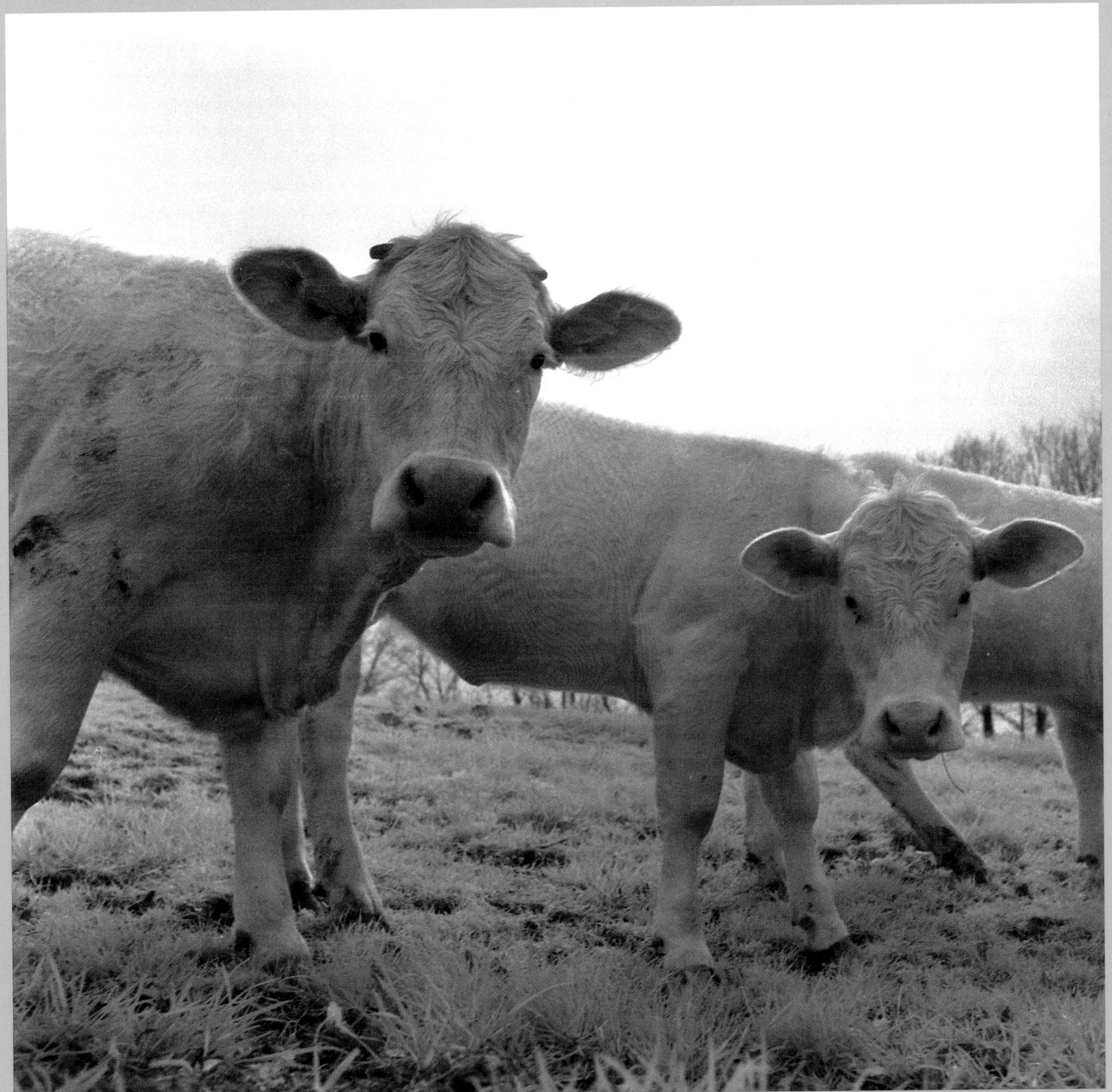

The Economics of Cows

by Vernon L. Smith

I was born in Wichita, Kansas, in 1927, and moved to a farm forty-five miles from there when I was five years old. This was 1932, in the depths of the Great Depression. In Kansas there is precious little wood except along the creeks. This was due to the countless years of lightning storms that kept the prairies burned off so that only grass, particularly blue stem "buffalo" grass, survived by resprouting from the roots after every burn. Blue stem is mostly gone now, but it is said that in a good year you had to be on horseback to see across the top of it.

As a boy, I learned when and how to milk cows and put them to pasture. But my most important job was to gather dried, sun-baked "cow chips." These were to be burned in our potbellied heating stove, and in our wood cookstove, along with some cottonwood and dried corncobs.

The early settlers had burned Bison chips, as had the Indians before them. Decades later I learned that the first Americans who crossed to Alaska on the land bridge from Siberia burned Mammoth chips. So I felt connected to those ancient peoples of 14,000 years ago.

I guess you could say that, thanks to those cow chips, I received some of my first lessons in economics.

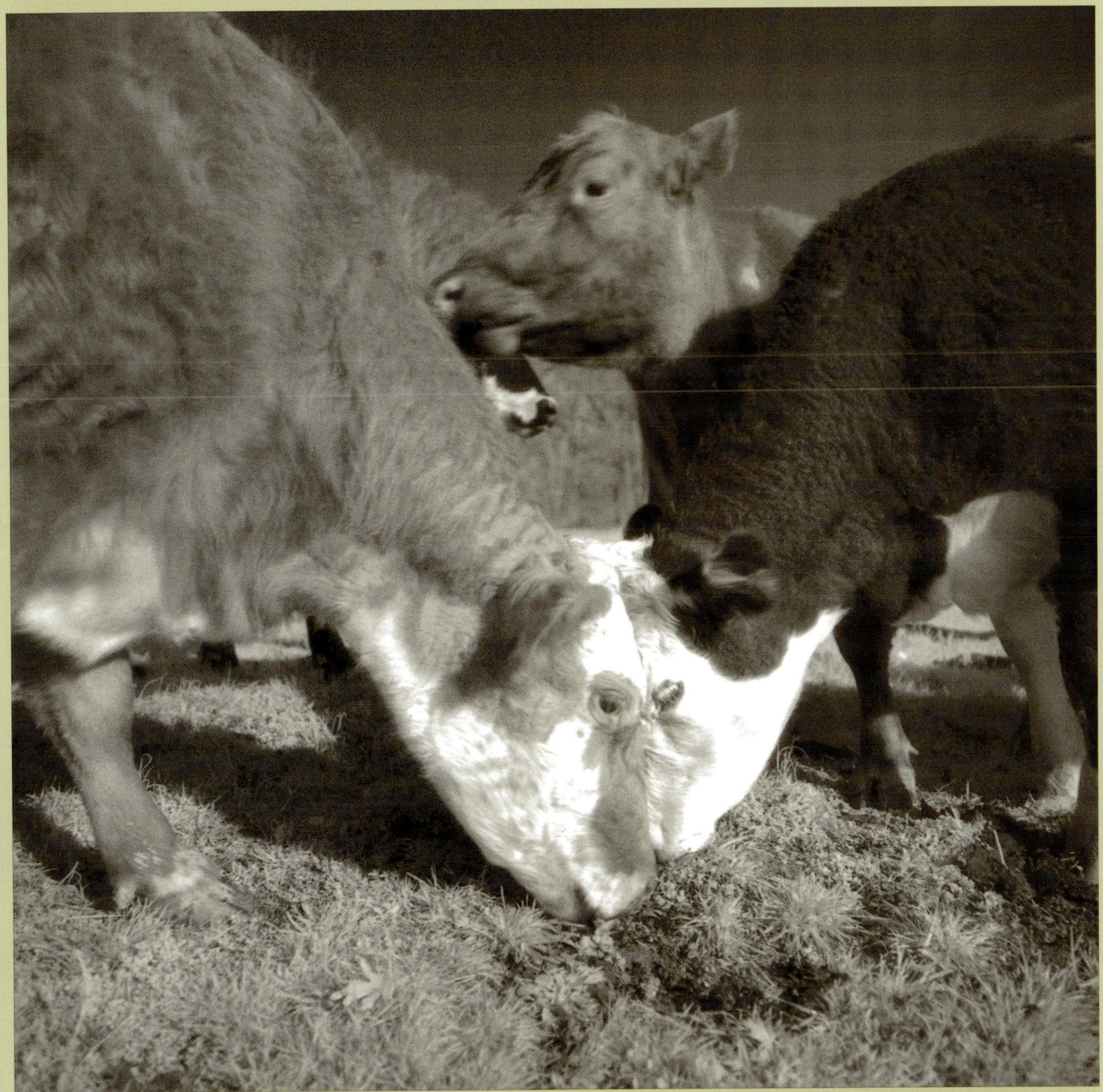

The Wisdom of Cows

A noisy cow gives little milk.
–Polish Proverb

The good cow gets sold in its own country.
–Maltese Proverb

Milk the cow, but do not pull off the udder.
–Greek Proverb

Before you milk a cow, tie it up.
–South African Proverb

Her horns are not heavy for a cow.
–Ethiopian Proverb

Whoever needs milk bows to the animal.
–Yiddish Proverb

The cow does not know the value of her tail till she has lost it.
–Danish Proverb

The cow gives good milk, but kicks over the pail.
–Old Proverb

The cow has no owner.
–Massai Proverb

The cow licks no strange calf.
–German Proverb

The cow must graze where she is tied.
–Sierra Leonean Proverb

The cow that's first up gets the first of the dew.
–British Proverb

It is better if the kick comes from a milk cow. And better an empty shed than a wicked cow. **–Bangladesh Proverb**

God keeps away flies from the tailless cow.
–Nigerian Proverb

The cow: God with a wet nose.
–Mosotho Proverb, Africa

The tail of the cow watches to the right and left.
–Wadchagga Proverb, Africa

Only when a tree has grown can you tie your cow to it.
–Jabo Proverb, Liberia

A cow which is dragged to Beijing is still a cow.
–Taiwanese Proverb

It is often that a cow does not take after its breed.
–Irish Proverb

No matter who you are you will never let your cow sink into the mud. **–South African Proverb**

The cow that does not eat with the oxen either eats before or after them. **–Galician Proverb**

Settling a dispute through the law is like losing a cow for the sake of a cat. **–Chinese Proverb**

If you are buying a cow, make sure that the price of the tail is included. **–Tamil Proverb**

Two farmers each claimed to own a certain cow. While one pulled on its head and the other on its tail, the cow was milked by a lawyer. **–Jewish Proverb**

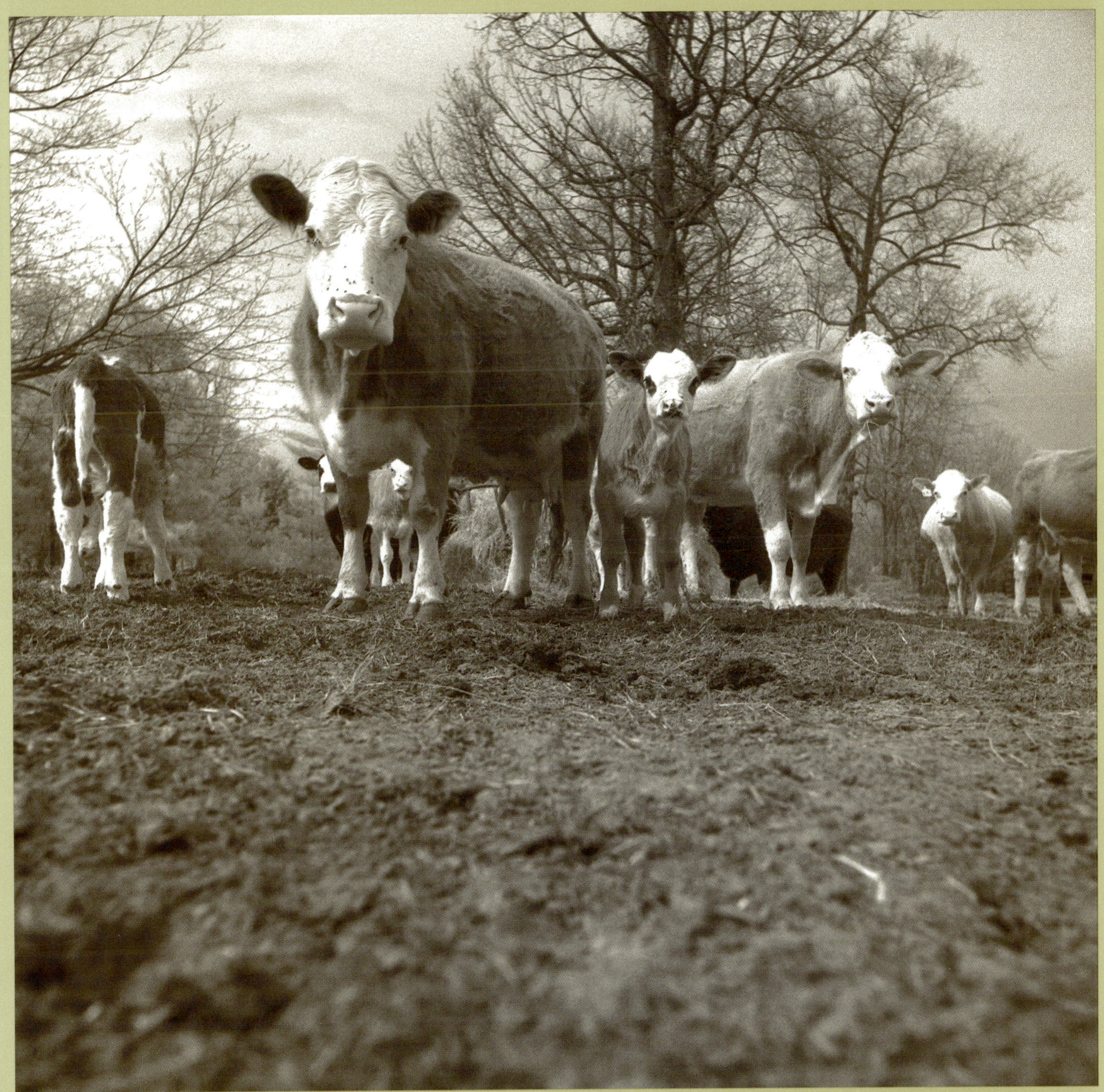

The Art of Cows

by Dave Prowse

I was born and raised in Bristol,England. Because I didn't grow up in a rural area, I didn't really have an opportunity to see cows parading about on farms. And I'm quite certain there were no cows in Darth Vader's childhood either.

But then I visited the city of Chicago a few years ago. To my amazement, hundreds of cows promenaded the streets of that city, as well as dotted the city centre. They were enchanting, a true crowd pleaser, with tourists stopping daily to stare at their bright colors and designs. As Darth Vader himself might have remarked, these cows were "Impressive, most impressive."

Of course, even a city boy like me could tell they weren't real, just life-size statues, works of art done by Chicago residents. Yet we all stood and gawked at them as if they might "moo" at any second, or perhaps even bolt through the streets. They had quite an effect on the visitors. Almost hypnotic. I had to wonder if real cows would stare at them too. Would they know the difference?

I suspect this is something only real cows will ever know. And they're not telling.

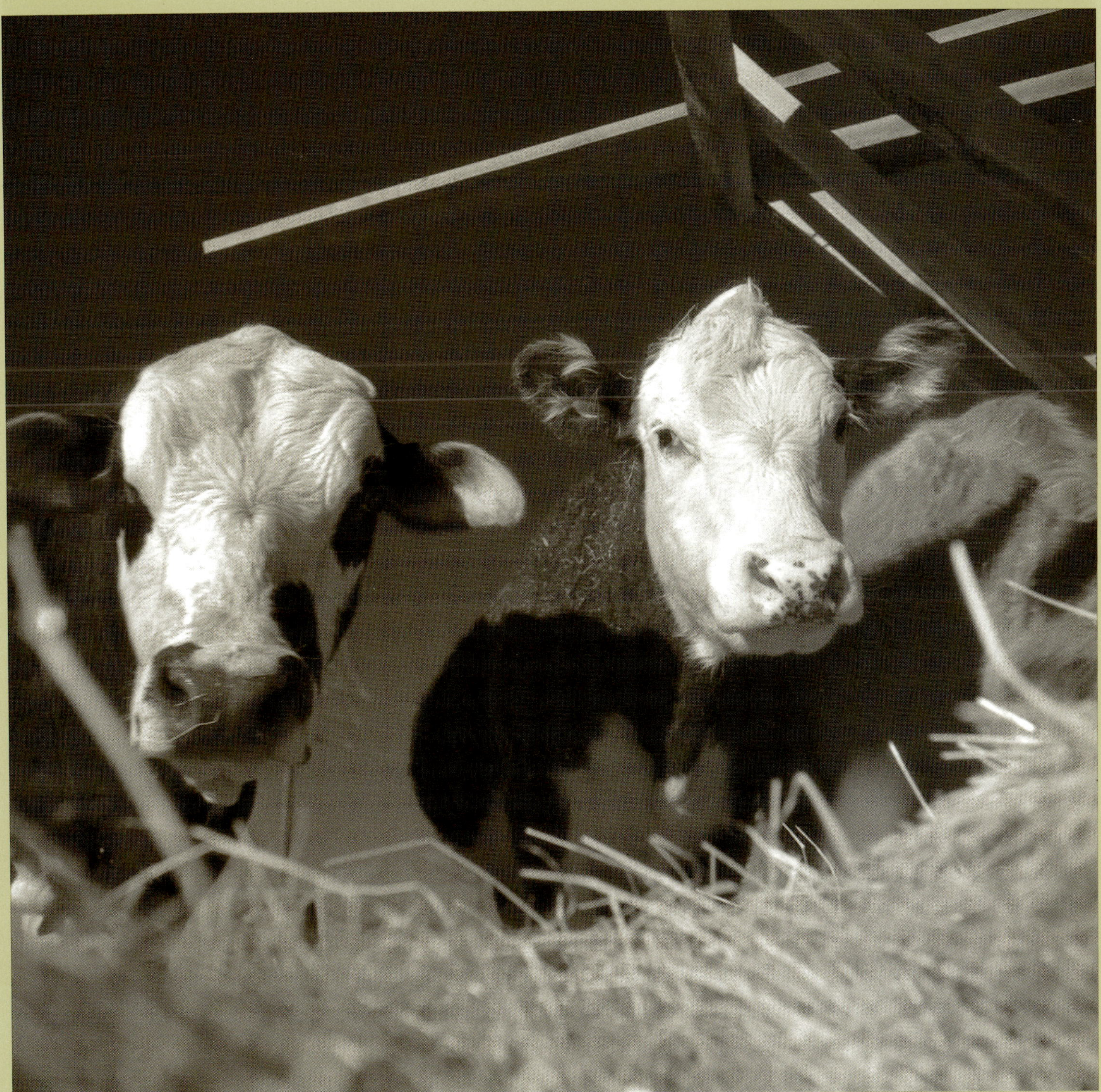

The Heroism of Cows

WELLINGTON, New Zealand—A farmer's wife who was swept away by floods in New Zealand yesterday had her life saved by a cow. Kim Riley praised the animal—known only as Number 569—and described it as "an ugly old tart." The area around Mrs. Riley's farm at Woodville, near Palmerston North, has been lashed by severe storms that have claimed two lives, washed away wooden houses and forced the evacuation of hundreds of North Island homes. Insurers put the cost of damage at 40 million. Mrs. Riley was leading in a herd of 350 cows in early morning darkness when they were caught in a torrent of floodwater.

"It was just amazing how the current picked me up," she said. "Before I knew it, I was being pushed along with the cows." Mrs. Riley said several of the panicking animals went over the top of her, leaving her badly bruised from their kicks. Then she saw that a group of cows had made its way to an outcrop of dry land. "I couldn't swim there, the current was too strong," she said. "I tried to grab a tree, but missed. I thought if I was washed into the main river, I would be gone. That's when I realized I was in real trouble. I thought most of the cows had abandoned me. They were strong swimmers and left me in their wake. But I looked back and saw one of the last cows bearing down on me, number 569. As she went by I threw my arm over her neck. She was strong, and the warmth that was coming from her was so reassuring. I just laid back and relaxed, and said, 'Take me home.'

When we actually hit hard ground, we both sat there quite exhausted, puffing and shaking. I could never have made it on my own. She's an old cow, an ugly old tart, but I'll have to say 'thank you' to her for saving my life."

February 18, 2004, from the *Telegraph,* United Kingdom.

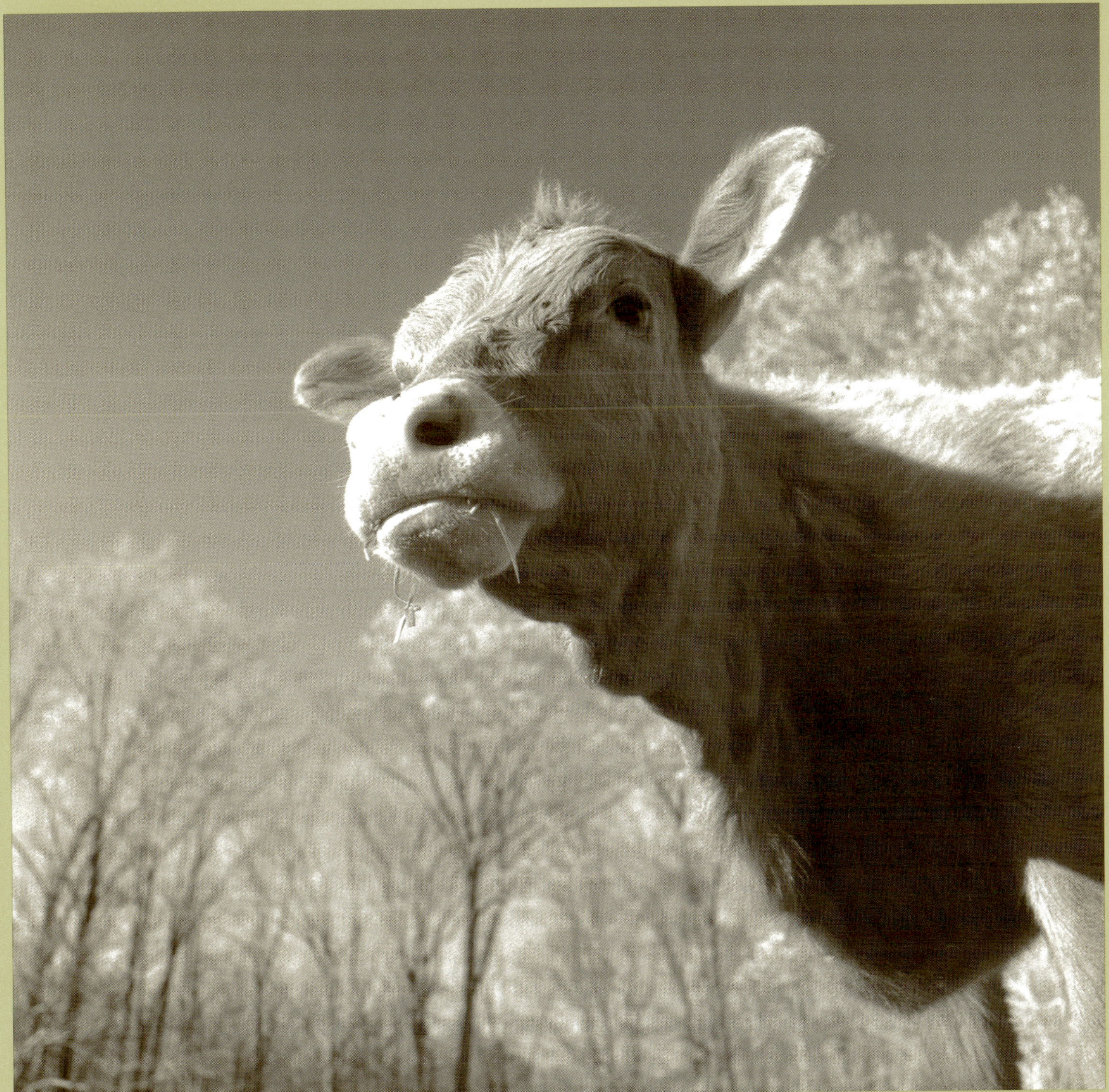

The Companionship of Cows

He wished, without reserve, that he was at home again making the endless rounds from the house to the barn, from the barn to the fields, from the fields to the barn, from the barn to the house. He remembered he had often cursed the brindle cow and her mates, and had sometimes flung milking stools. But, from his present point of view, there was a halo of happiness about each of their heads, and he would have sacrificed all the brass buttons on the continent to have been enabled to return to them. He told himself that he was not formed for a soldier.

From *The Red Badge of Courage,* by Stephen Crane.

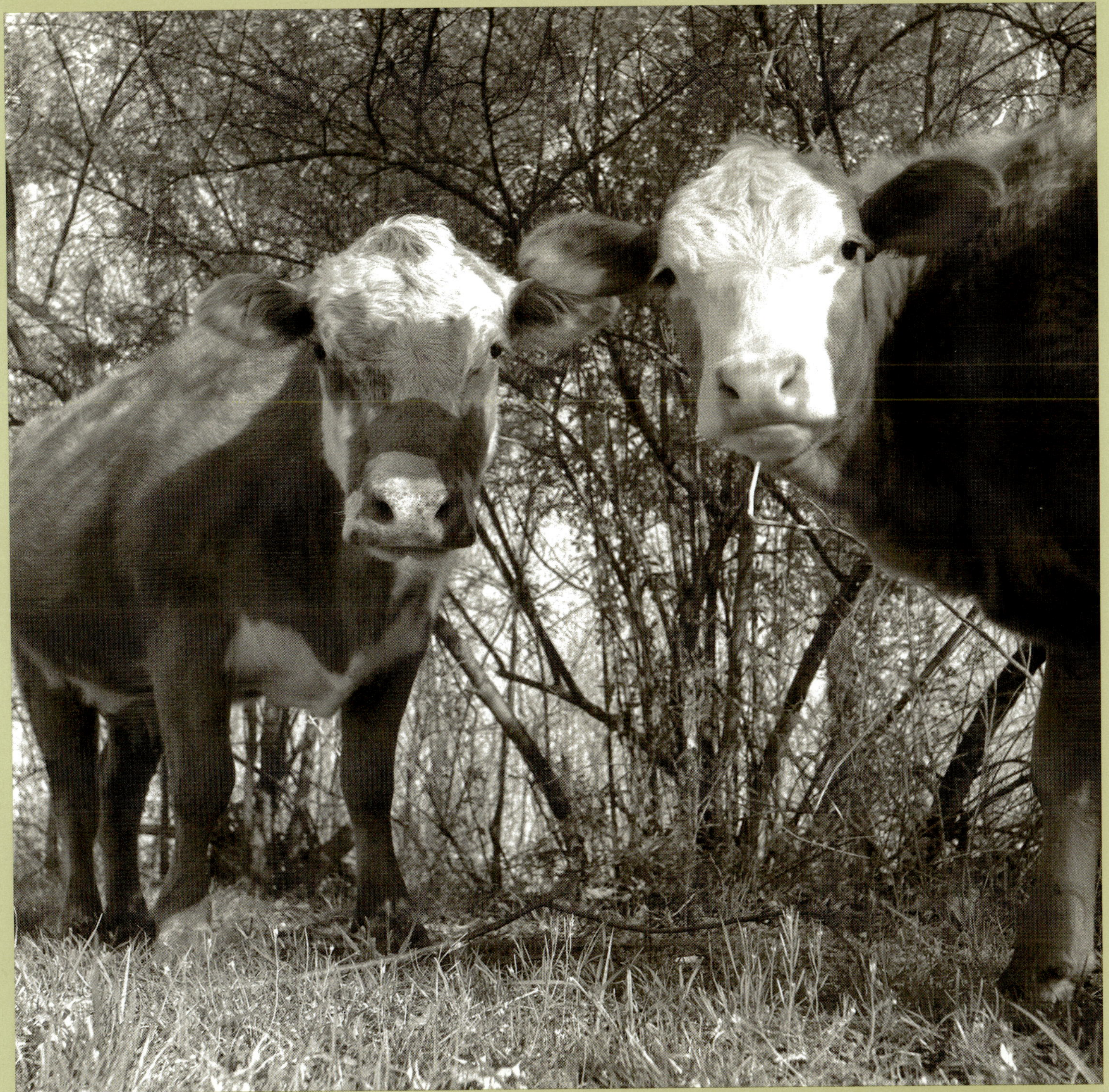

The Lure of Cows

by Wesley McNair

I got the idea for this poem when I was reading an account in a local newspaper about a town historian who'd run across the story of a drunk man who was shingling his roof one afternoon, and at a certain moment stood up, announced he was going out to fetch the cows for milking and walked off the roof, killing himself—a funny story, at least it was told as a funny story, in that famously grim Yankee humor. Nobody knows anything else about this man (I had to give him his name, Shorty Towers) except that he lived his life in northern New England, just as farming was passing out of existence ...

The Last Time Shorty Towers Fetched the Cows

In the only story we have
of Shorty Towers, it is five o'clock
and he is dead drunk on his roof
deciding to fetch the cows. How
he got in this condition, shingling
all afternoon, is what the son-in-law,
the one who made the back pasture
into a golf course, can't figure out. So,
with an expression somewhere between shock
and recognition, he just watches Shorty
pull himself up to his not-so-
full height, square his shoulders,
and sigh that small sigh, as if caught
once again in an invisible swarm
of bees. Let us imagine, in that moment
just before he turns to the roof's edge
and the abrupt end of the joke
which is all anyone thought to remember
of his life, Shorty is listening
to what seems to be the voice
of a lost heifer, just breaking
upward. And let us think that when he walks
with such odd purpose down that hill
jagged with shingles, he suddenly feels it
open into the wide, incredibly green
meadow where all the cows are.

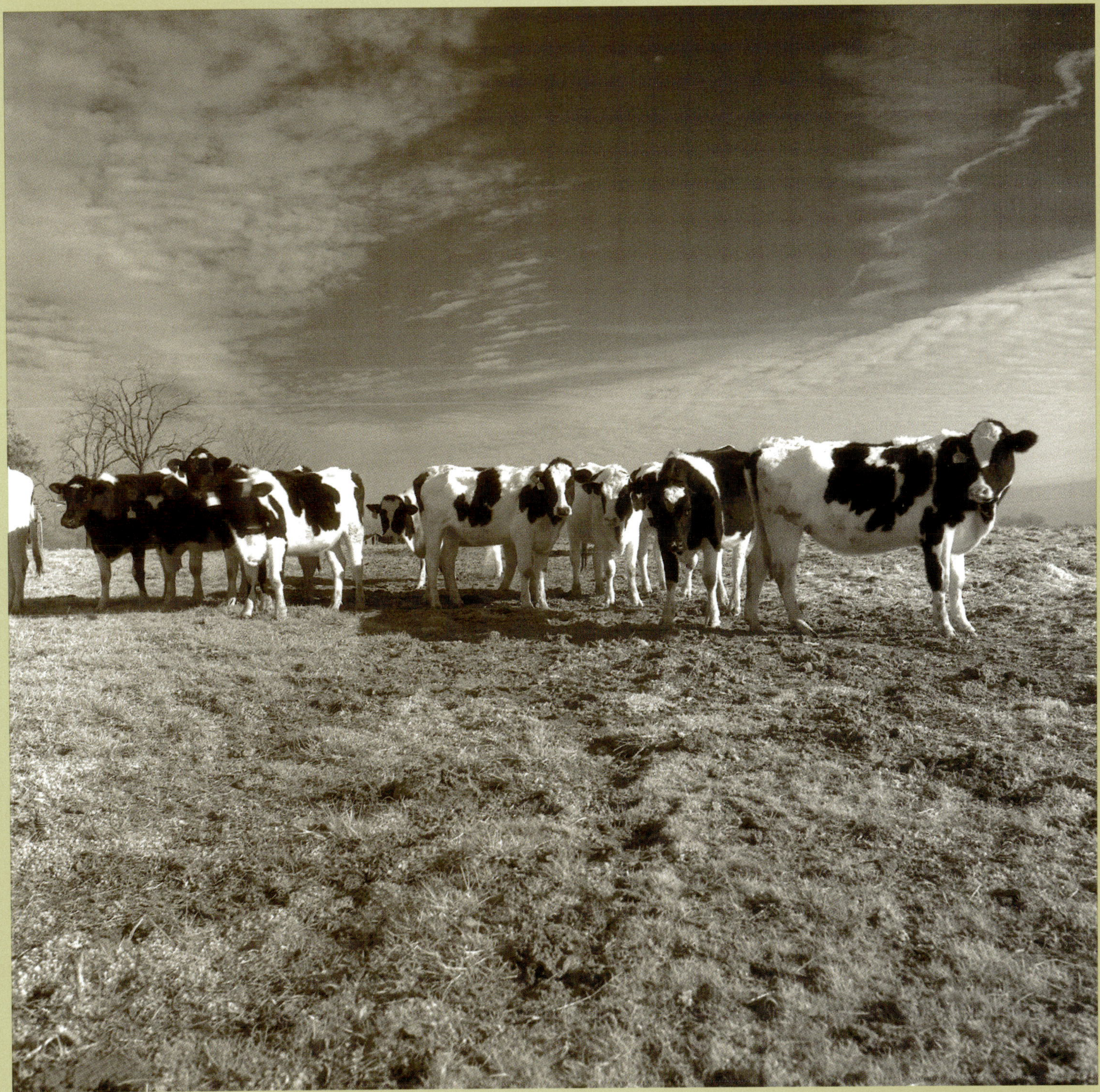

The Afterlife of Cows

by Jack Sage

In the 1850s, Andrew Byrd constructed a dam at the outlet of Steilacoom Lake (originally called Byrd Lake, in Washington state.) Below this dam, Byrd had built a grist mill for grinding wheat into flour. Later, he added a lumber mill and a slaughterhouse for the convenience of the local farmers.

One day a mentally disturbed man, J.M. Bates, lost his cow, which was one of his few possessions. Bates went to Steilacoom in search of the missing animal. While in one of the town's saloons on Commercial Street, he met up with an enemy of Byrd. This informant falsely told Bates that Andrew Byrd had taken his cow to the slaughterhouse and butchered it.

Bates encountered Byrd and asked what had happened to his cow. Byrd didn't know what it was all about and told Bates to look elsewhere for his animal.

Several days later Byrd came to the post office in Steilacoom to pick up his weekly mail. When Byrd entered the post office, Bates shot Andrew Byrd twice. Byrd died the next night as a result of his wounds. Before he died, Byrd asked that J. M. Bates not be harmed since he was mentally ill.

Sheriff Peter Judson locked Bates in the Steilacoom jail. Early the next morning, January 23, 1863, a mob of more than a hundred men stormed the jail. After locking up the sheriff, the mob dragged Bates out of his cell. A rope was found and J. M. Bates was hanged in the nearby Henry Murray barn.

The man who falsely accused Andrew Byrd of stealing Bates' cow immediately fled to Oregon. The missing cow was never found.

It is claimed that on moonlit nights, the ghost of J. M. Bates, with a noose still around his neck, may be seen carrying a long rope. It's said that if you are very quiet, you may hear him calling out for his lost animal, his beloved cow.

It might only be the wind blowing, but we will never be sure.

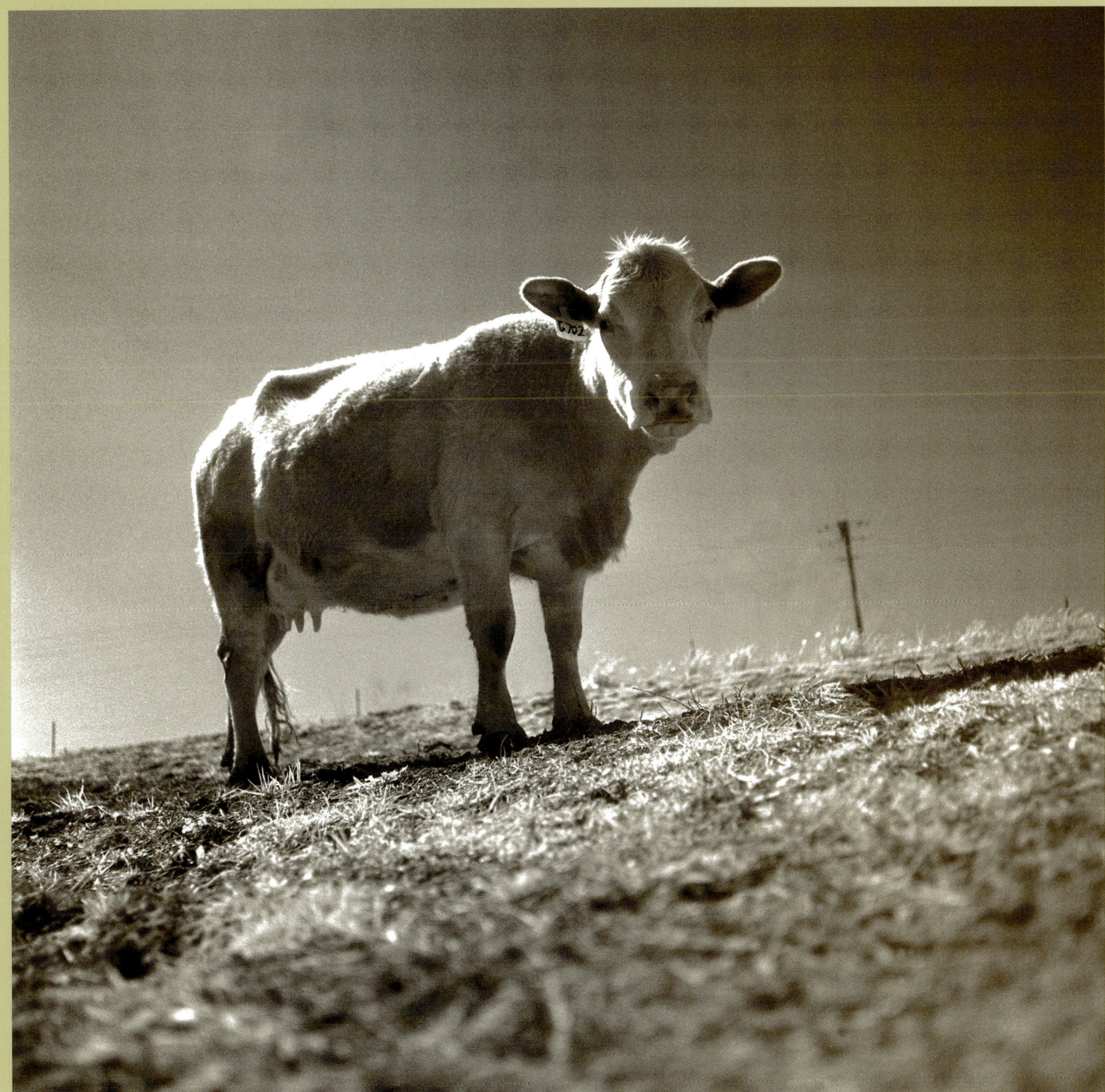
6702

The Music of Cows

by Tanya Tucker

Cows are great country & western music fans. They love the old songs about Texas, Oklahoma, Wyoming, and Montana. They especially love songs about the prairie. Traditional country & western music keeps cows settled down and happy. That's why cowboys sang it to them out on the trail, on all those cattle drives. And it's why, even after rock 'n' roll became popular, cowboys never tried to serenade their herd with a rock song. They knew darn well it would result in a full-out stampede.

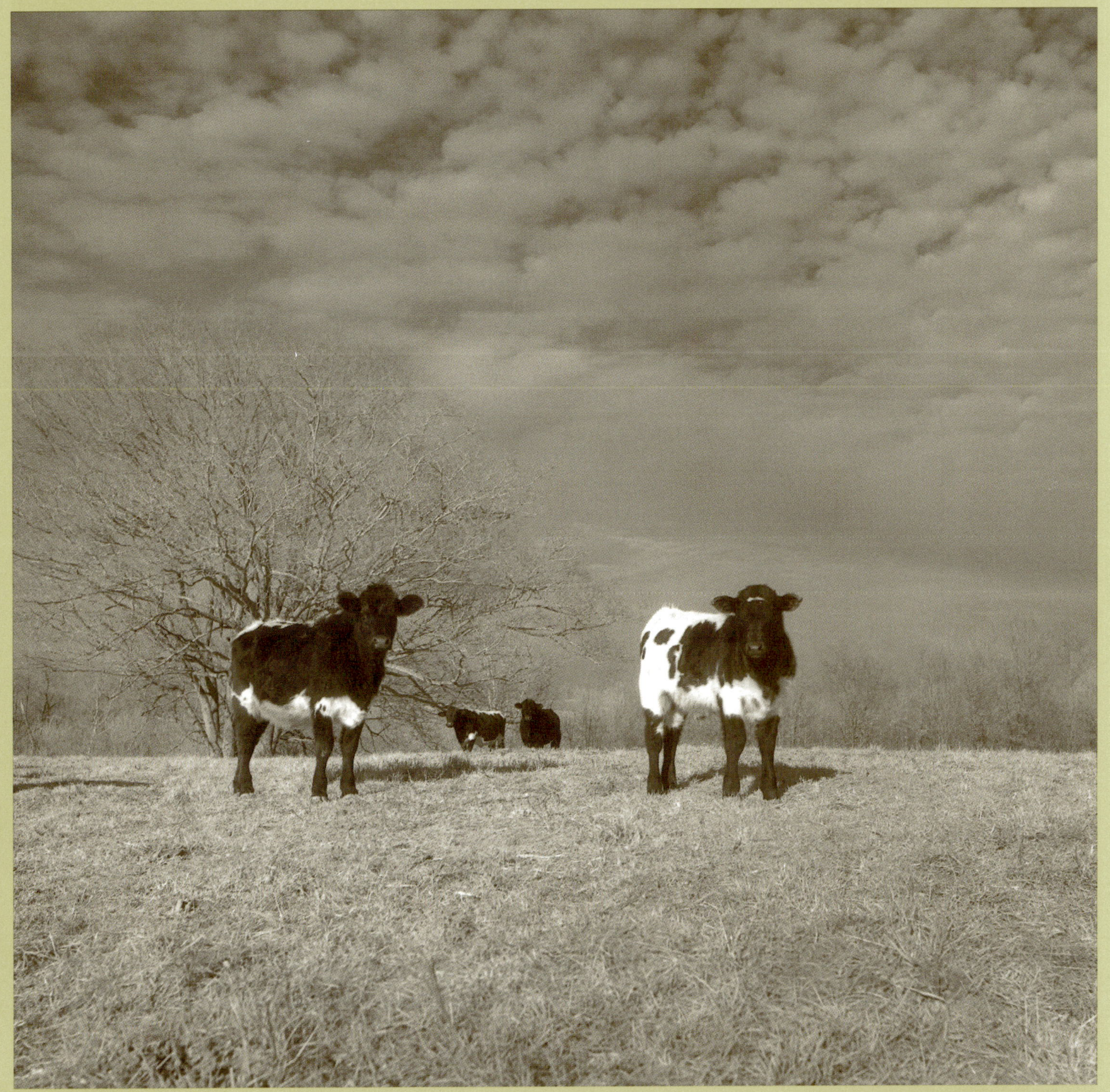

The Criminology of Cows

by Sue McClure

It's not every day that a criminal gets collared by a cow. In fact, this ranks as number one in "the most unusual captures" I've covered in my twenty-four years as a journalist.

Lawmen in rural Tennessee had launched a massive manhunt for Parker Ray Elliott, who was accused of shooting and killing his wife and daughter. They received several tips to narrow their search, but the final nod, so to speak, came from some cows gathered near a barn.

As Ellie May, the bloodhound tracking Elliott, entered the field, her handler noticed the cows weren't looking in his direction.

"I knew those cows should have been looking at me, since I had just come into the area," said Shane Petty. "But they were looking over into the woods, so I knew that's where Parker Ray Elliot was."

You see, Petty, who is a special operations officer for Tennessee State Parks, also has a degree in agriculture.

"I'm an old farm boy," he said.

It paid off in this manhunt.

The suspect was ultimately "Busted by Bovines."

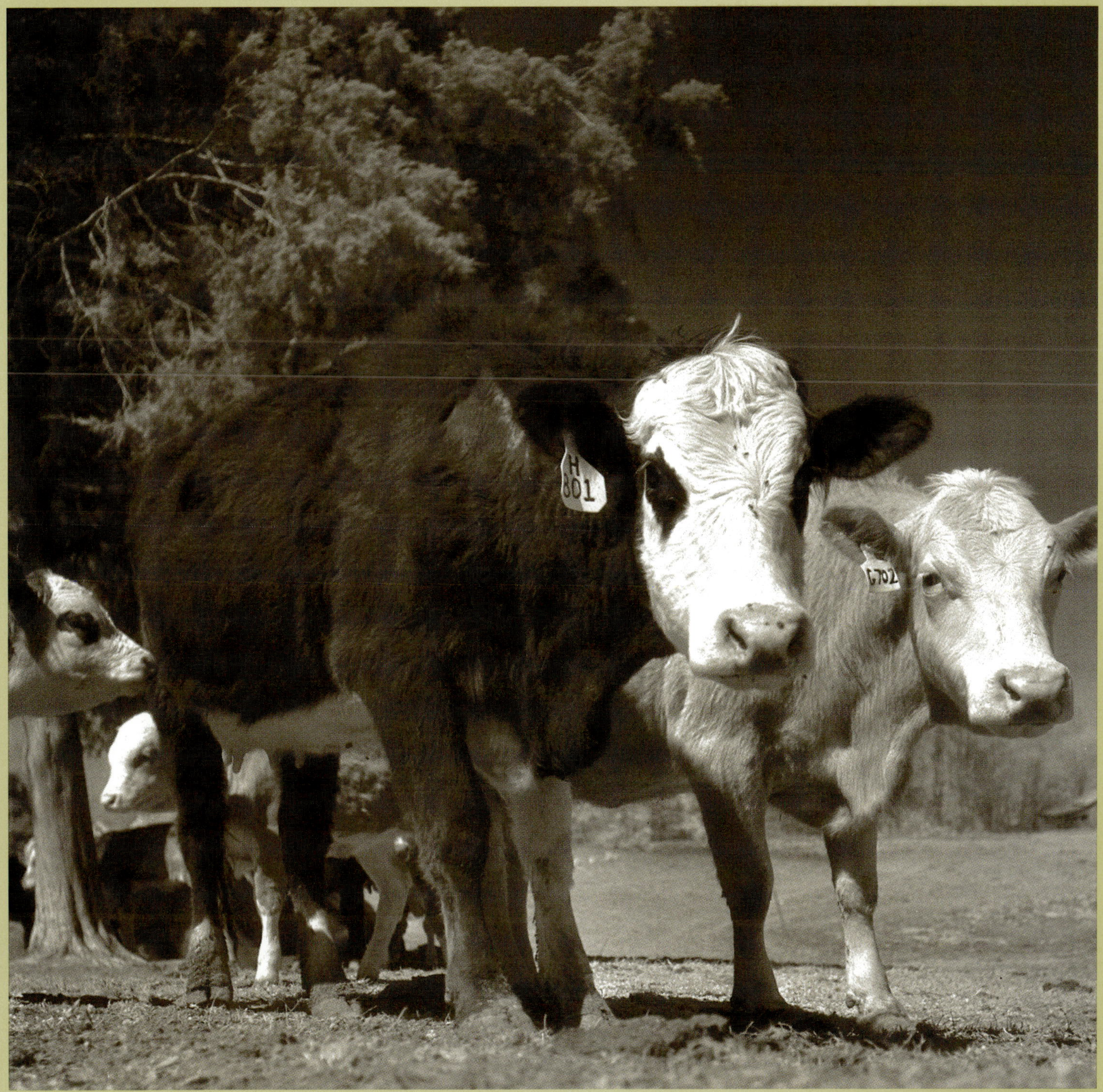
H
801
G702

The Uniqueness of Cows

by Laura Gilpin

At least once a year throughout my childhood, my father insisted on making a family pilgrimage out of the flat lands of Indianapolis to the hills of Brown County to see fall foliage or the redbuds blooming in the spring. I always considered these trips tedious and boring until we discovered an old jailhouse in Nashville, Indiana, that had become a museum. I don't remember how old I was—maybe nine or ten—when I first saw the taxidermied two-headed calf housed in the museum, but I remember being haunted by his eyes. After that, I looked forward to our annual pilgrimages, and the opportunity to visit this strange and beautiful creature.

The Two-Headed Calf

Tomorrow when the farm boys find this
freak of nature, they will wrap his body
in newspaper and carry him to the museum.

But tonight he is alive and in the north
field with his mother. It is a perfect
summer evening: the moon rising over
the orchard, the wind in the grass. And
as he stares into the sky, there are
twice as many stars as usual.

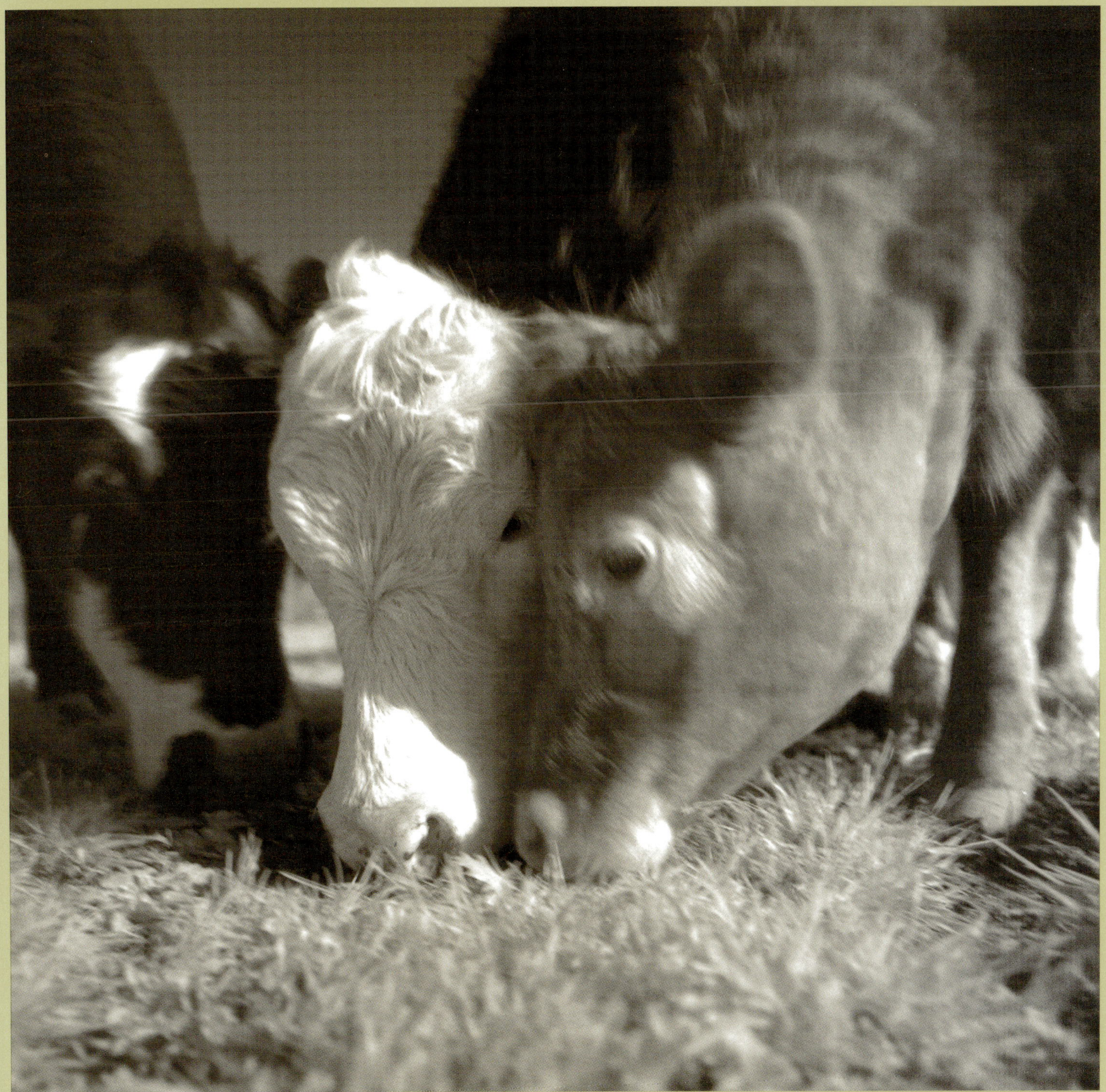

The Folklore of Cows

If a farmer's plow should kill a daddy longlegs, then the cows will certainly go dry.

If the bull leads the cows to pasture, expect rain; if the cows precede the bull, the weather will be uncertain.

Icelandic folklore states that if the first calf born during the winter is white, then the winter will be a miserable one.

Before a storm, cows will lie down and refuse to go out to pasture.
(Some people still say they can forecast storms by glancing at cows in a field.)

In Scotland, milk was left out for the "wee folk," or fairies, so that cows would give milk all summer.

In Irish folklore, witches are often known to steal milk from cows by turning themselves into hares.

In some Celtic areas, it was believed that cows should be informed of their owner's death. Otherwise, the cows would sense that something was very wrong, and they would sicken and most likely die.

In Poland, there were days when evil powers were most active, two being St. Lucia Day (December 13th) and Christmas Eve. On these two days, witches used magic to steal milk from the cows. To do this, they put magic herbs in the stable, or attempted to steal something belonging to the house. As a result, no guests or visitors were allowed in any homes on these days.

According to Irish folklore, in the winter, the milk goes to the cow's horns.

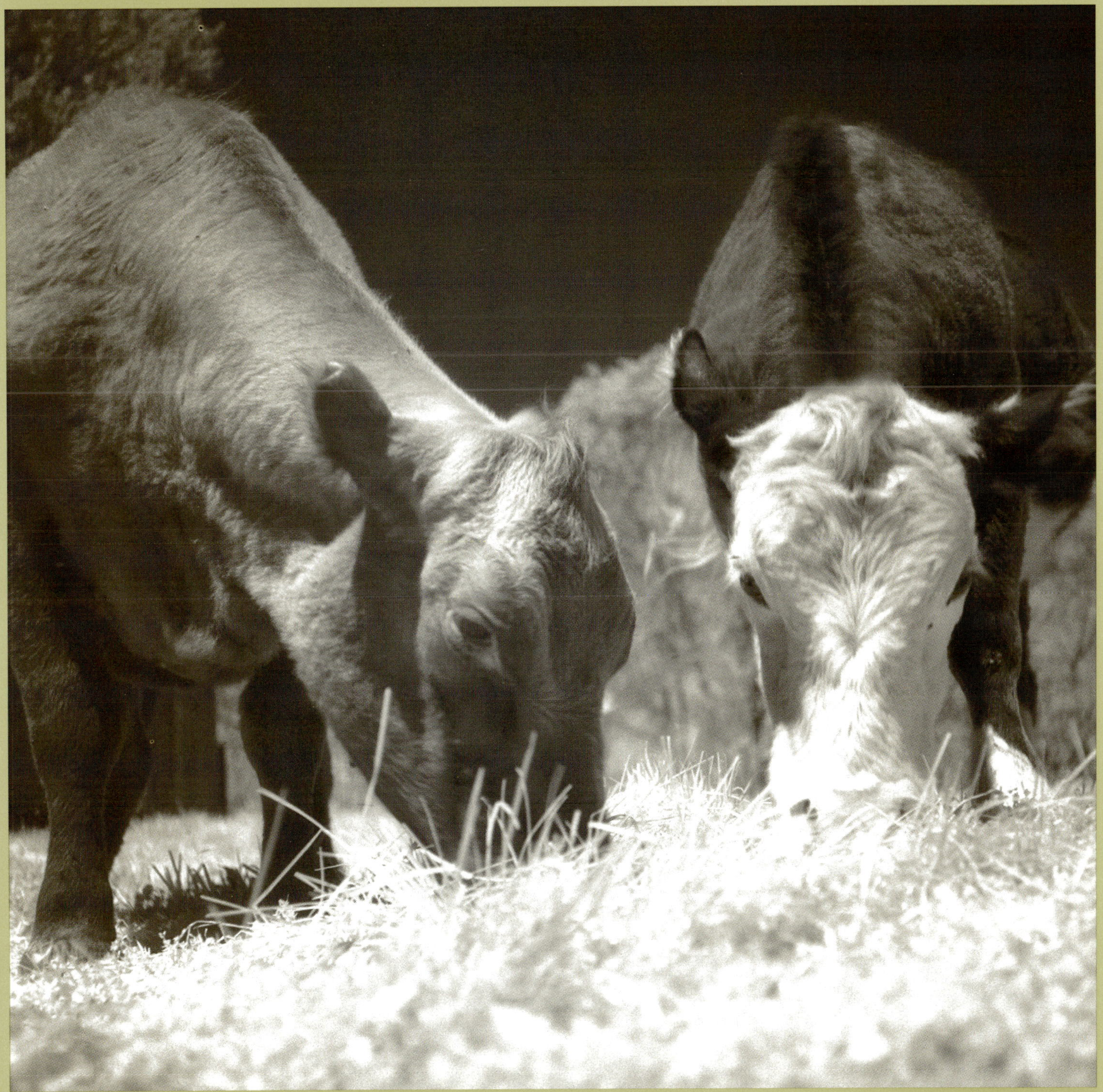

The Conversation of Cows

There's nothing like sitting back and talking to your cows.

Russell Crowe, the actor, on why he misses Australia, *US Weekly* magazine.

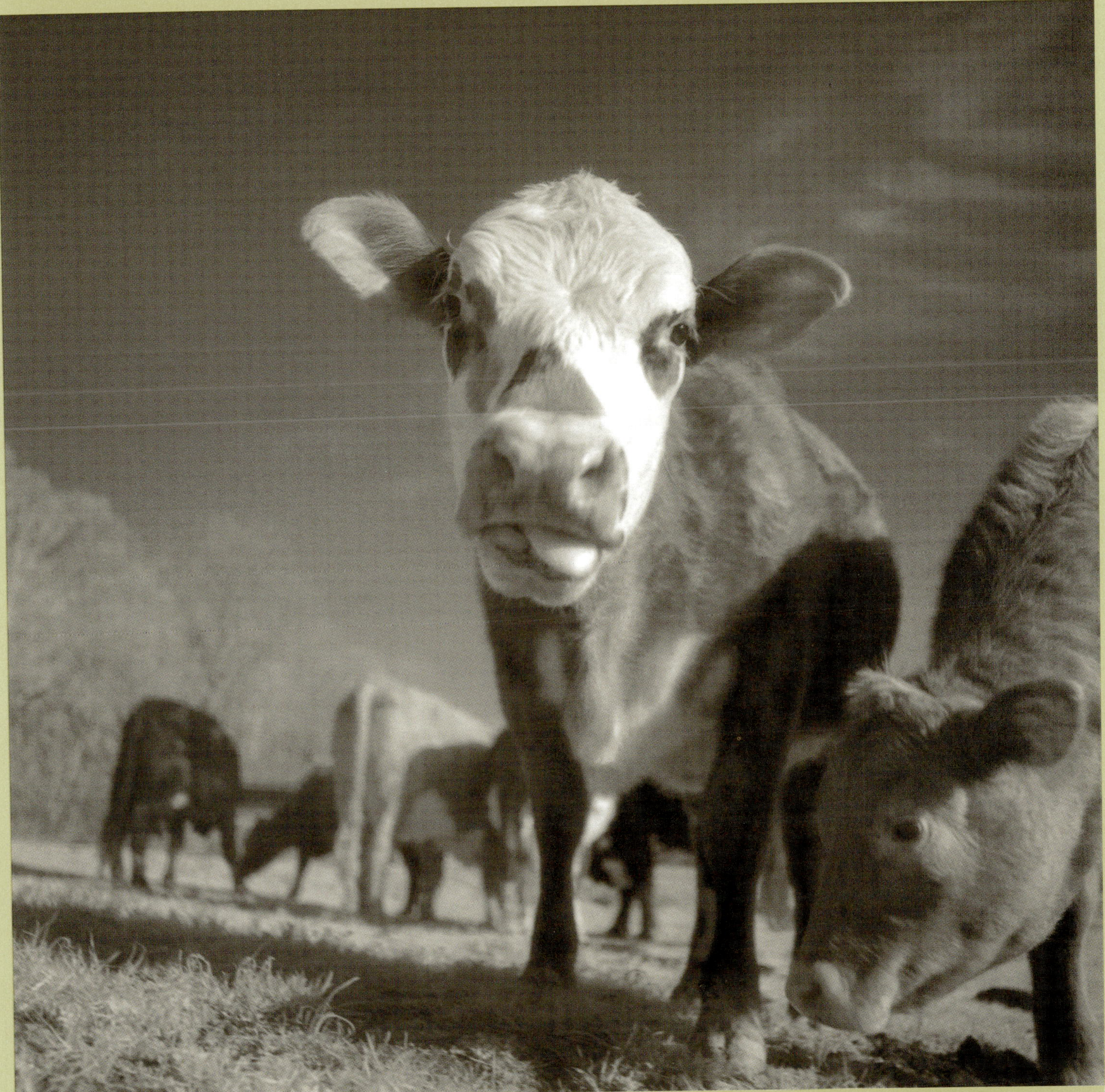

The Teachership of Cows

by Shirley Skeel

Jeff Byers has an unconventional solution for world strife. "If everyone had a cow, the world would be a more peaceful place," he says. It's not exactly a workable plan in practice. But Byers does what he can to introduce harassed city folk to this slow and serene vegetarian. This particular day he is at Bessie Carmichael School, a squat, terra cotta-colored building south of Mission Street in San Francisco, where many Filipino, Hispanic, and Cambodian children spend their days. His big Chevy truck has pulled into the schoolyard, towing an even bigger white van, marked "Dairy Council of California, Mobile Classroom." He opens the rear doors and hauls out a bucket of carrots and artichokes, then leads out a long-legged calf and ties it behind the van. He's just in time. The school doors swing open and the wall of noise that only 200 excited kids can make pours into the playground. Two by two, the children plop down before the van for a quick lesson in bovine etiquette.

"Call me Mr. Jeff. I want *no noise.* Cows don't like noise," says Byers, who was a teacher before he became an instructor in the Dairy Council's nutrition education program. "And the cow behaves like a cow. If she acts like a cow, *do not* laugh at her. She'll chew and she'll gulp and she may stick her tongue in her nose. *Pleeease* do not laugh at her."

He opens the van's side doors. Electra, or Ellie for short, is big. Huge. Maybe eight feet long and five feet high. Black and white and a mother of three, she is an 1,800-pound Holstein heifer with the hips of an army sergeant and the eyes of a saint. The children go silent. Two girls put their hands over their mouths. Jeff scans the kids' faces, then the lesson begins. Ellie, offered a fistful of alfalfa, demonstrates how you tackle the ritual of eating when—like the deer, camel, goat, and giraffe—you have four stomachs. Thirty-nine chews, a gulp, a pause, and the food slides back up for a second work-over.

The kids learn that Ellie walks on two toes, has 32 teeth, and takes nine months to give birth. And she's not stupid. Every day, Saturday and Sunday included, she waits at the gate of Moon Glow Dairy, at Moss Landing on Monterey Bay, for Jeff to take her to school. She is affectionate, patient, and never gets riled. Can the same be said for kids?

Jeff decides to find out. He grabs a teat and squirts a stream of warm milk into the front row. The children screech and reel in horror. Many did not know milk comes from a cow. But they do now, and all because Jeff Byers takes cows to some 135 schools a year.

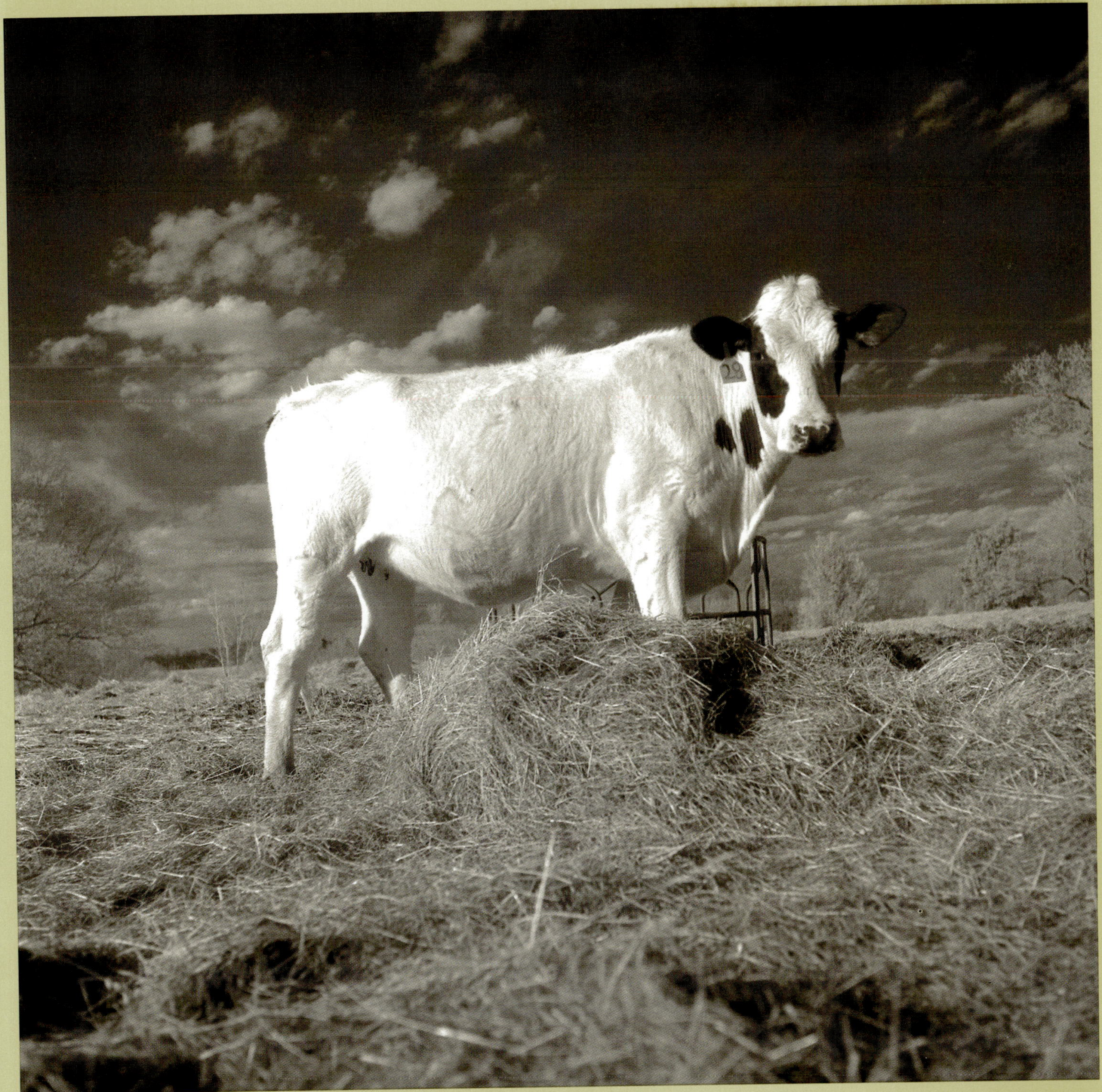
29

The Diplomacy of Cows

I love to watch my seven cows
In meads of buttercups abrowse,
With guilded knees;
But even more I love to see
Them chew the cud so tranquilly
In twilight ease.

Each is the image of content
From fragrant hours in clover spent,
'Mid leaf and bud;
As up and down without a pause
Mechanically move their jaws
To chew the cud.

Friend, there's a hope for me and you:
Let us resolve to chew and chew
With molars strong;
The man who learns to masticate
With patience may control his fate,
His life prolong.

In salivation is salvation:
So if some silly little nation
Should bathe in blood,
Let's take a lesson from the cow,
And learn in life's long gloaming how
To chew the cud.

—Robert W. Service

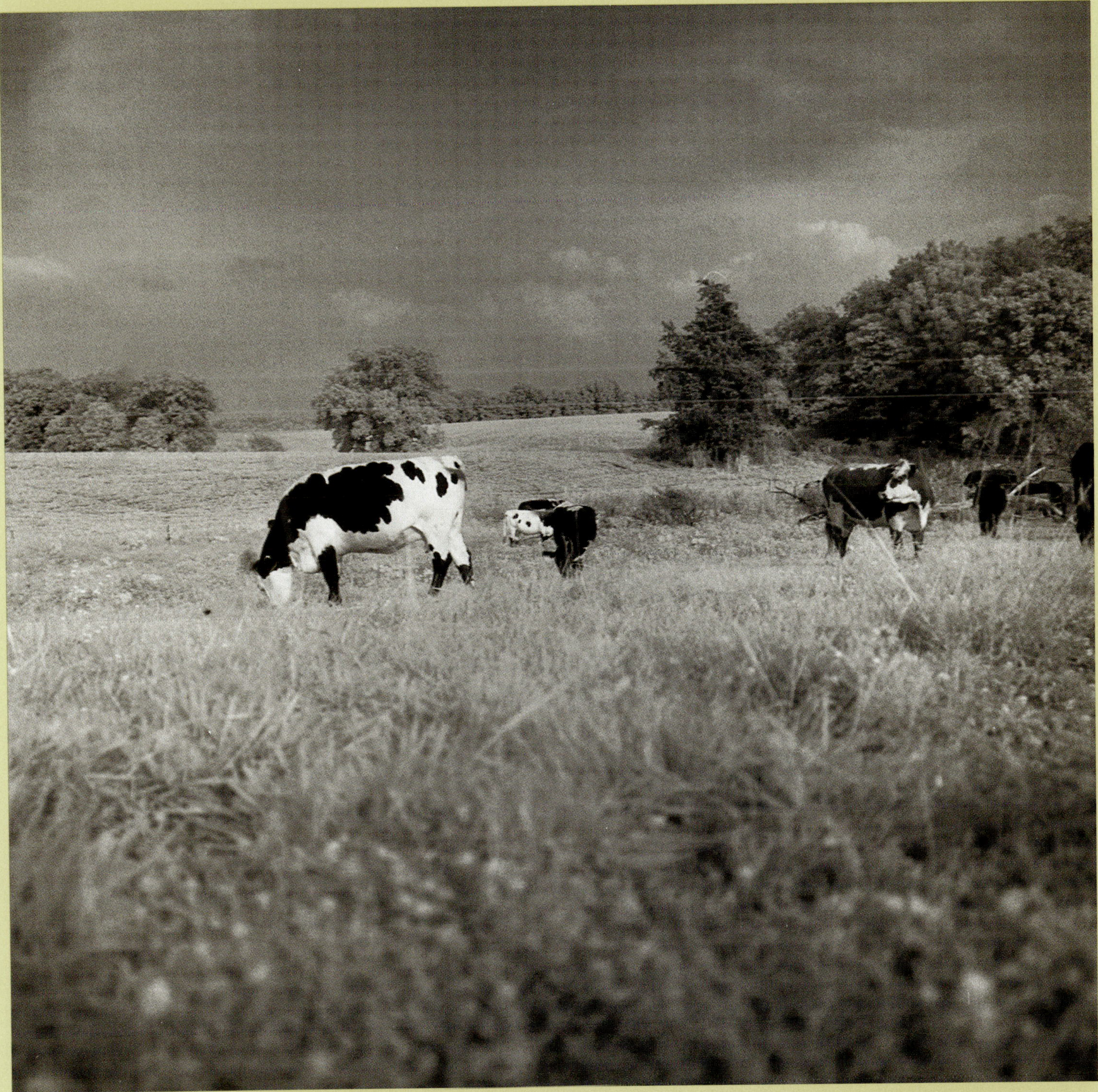

The Phraseology of Cows

HOW NOW, BROWN COW?
"Brown cow" was an eighteenth-century description for a barrel of beer. The phrase probably originated as a way of calling out for another round of drink. The barrel might be obsolete, but the saying lives on. Nowadays, it means "how are things going?"

WHY BUY A COW WHEN YOU CAN GET THE MILK FOR FREE?
Why pay for something that you can get for nothing?

AS STEEP AS A COW'S FACE.
Extremely steep and hazardous. Be careful climbing!

HOLY COW!
An exclamation that denotes major excitement.

BIG ENOUGH TO CHOKE A COW.
Very big, what else?

COW JUICE.
This would be milk, of course.

DARK AS THE INSIDE OF A COW'S BELLY.
In case you've never looked, it's very dark in there.

IT'S COMING DOWN LIKE A COW PISSING ON A FLAT ROCK.
It's raining really, *really* hard. Get an umbrella.

CASH COW.
An investment or business venture that has a steady profit or income, such as a cow that yields a regular supply of milk.

THAT'S THE TUNE THE OLD COW DIED OF ...
This is when you've heard a song so many times, it makes you ill to hear it again.

A SACRED COW.
A possession you cherish; or a person or inanimate object that is immune to criticism.

DON'T HAVE A COW.
Don't get mad, made popular again by Bart Simpson.

TILL THE COWS COME HOME.
This is a very long time, so don't wait up.

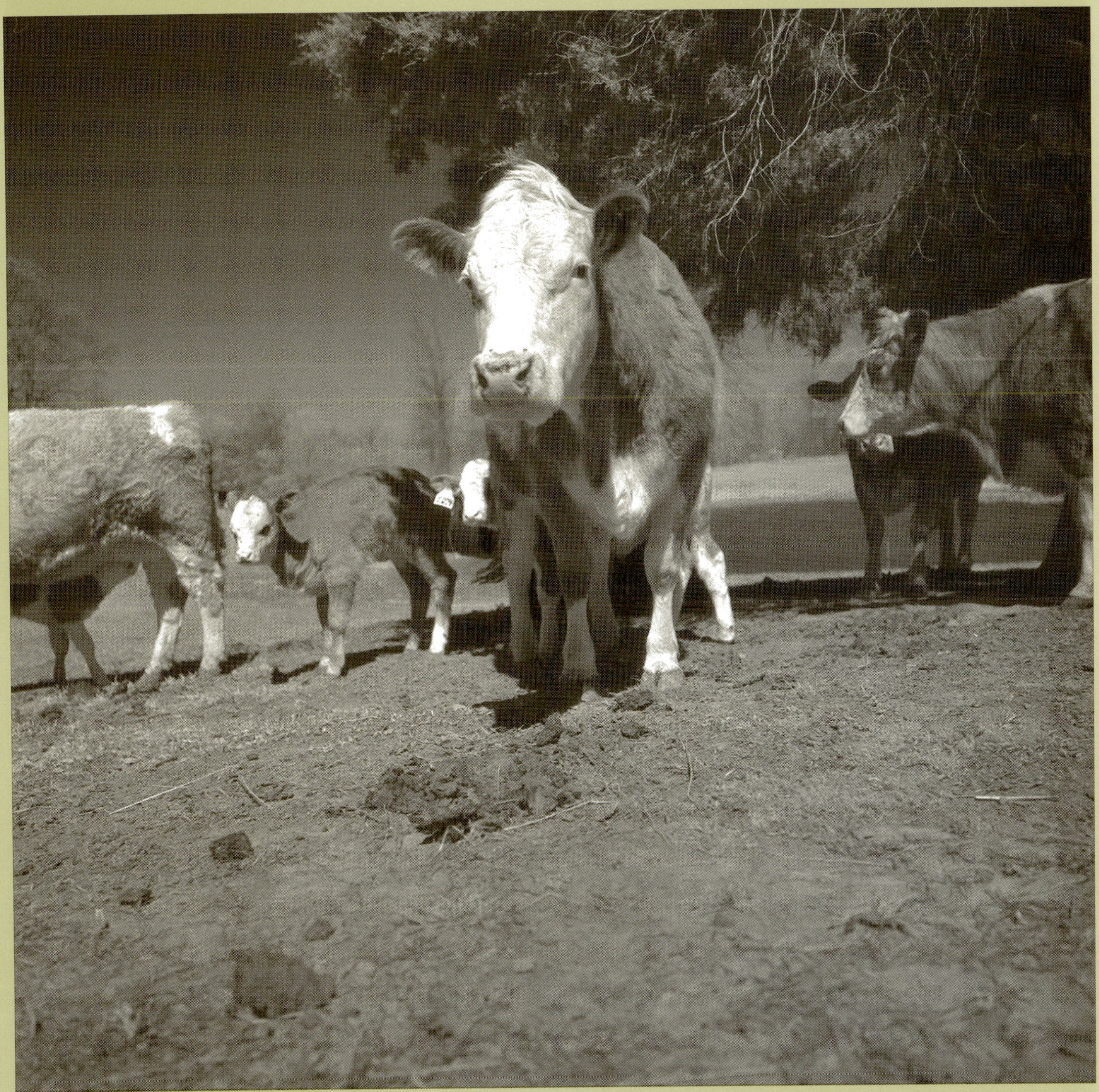

The Reincarnation of Cows

by Bill Anderson

I was riding in the car with Johnny Cash, on our way to a concert engagement in Michigan, back in the early sixties. Suddenly, Johnny directed the driver to pull off the road, turn off the engine, and let him look out the rear window at a field full of grazing cows. Nobody dared ask Johnny why he wanted to look at the field of cows. It was a given that Mr. Cash could look at whatever Mr. Cash wanted to look at, whenever he wanted to look at it.

The driver did as he was told. Johnny lowered the glass on the right-hand side of the jet-black Cadillac, stared at the cows for a while, then briefly got out and walked over by the fence. He pondered the cows from a closer point of view, then turned and climbed back into the back seat of the car, instructing the driver to resume the trip. Nobody said a word for the longest time. Finally, Johnny spoke up. "Well, he wasn't there," he said.

Our curiosity was certainly piqued. We all wanted to know who wasn't where. Johnny said calmly, "Johnny Horton. He always said that when he died he was going to come back someday reincarnated as a cow. I had a feeling he might have been out there in that field, but I checked carefully. He wasn't there."

The Stubbornness of Cows

Ralph Waldo Emerson knew poetry, science, history, and philosophy. But he knew nothing of putting a female calf into the barn. His son Edward helped by grabbing an ear while the philosopher pushed from the rear. But the heifer was having none of it. The more Emerson shoved, and the redder his face became, the more the calf pushed back. Man and animal had reached a stalemate when suddenly an Irish servant girl happened by and saw what was taking place. Amused, and knowledgeable far beyond history and philosophy, she stuck her finger into the calf's mouth. The calf, thinking the girl was its mother or the next best thing, sweetly followed her into the barn. Emerson went into his house, washed his hands, and then wrote in his journal of the scene he'd just witnessed.

From *The Life of Ralph Waldo Emerson* by Richard Garnett.

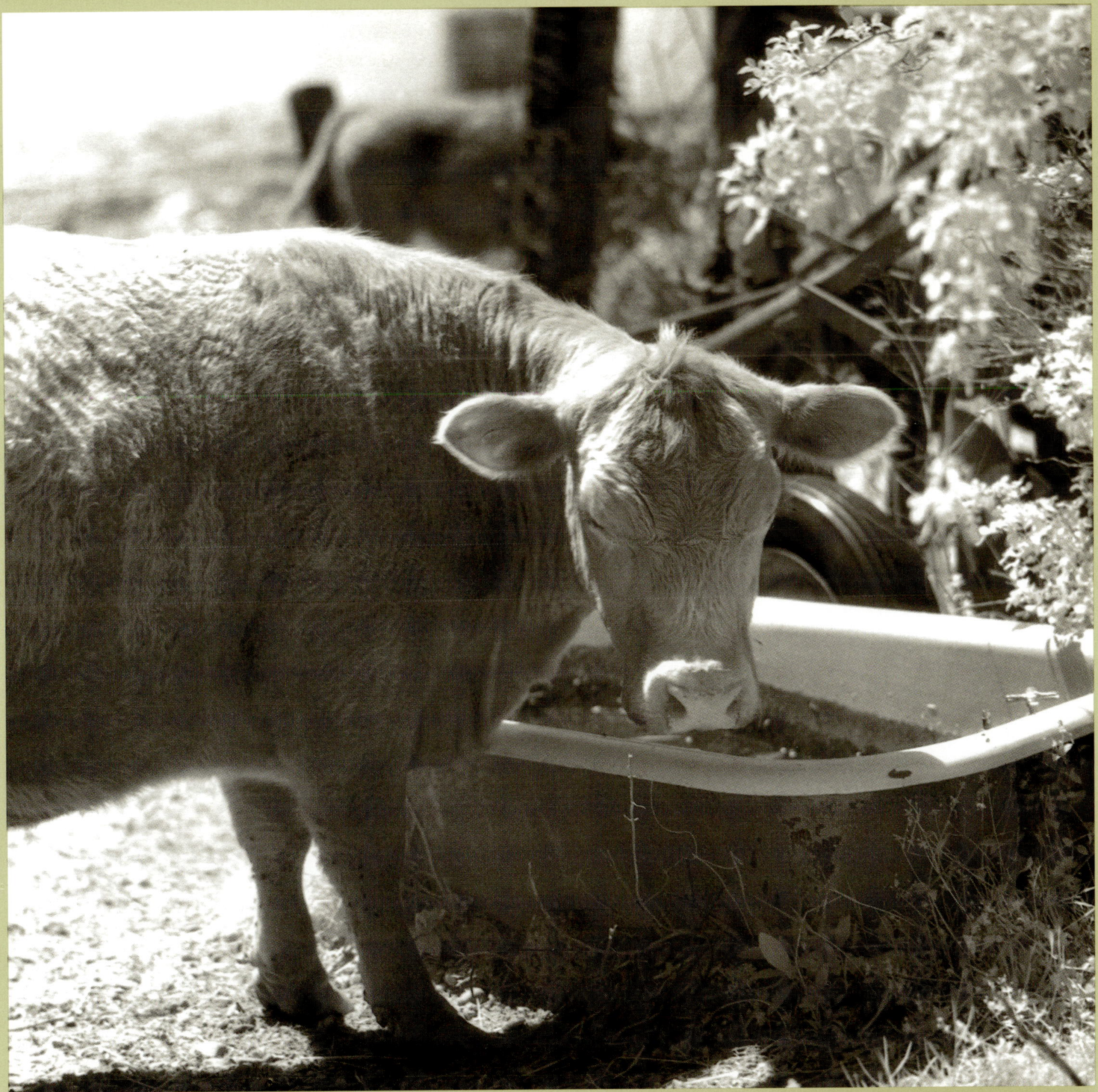

The Wanderlust of Cows

I wonder if I am here (Italy), or if I am just going to bed at the Ranch (Taos). Perhaps looking in Montgomery Ward's catalogue, and drinking moonshine and hot water, since it is cold. Go out and look if the chickens are shut up warm: if the horses are in sight: if Susan, the black cow, has gone to her nest among the trees, for the night. The cows don't eat much at night. But Susan will wander in the moon. The moon makes her uneasy.

From "A Little Moonshine with Lemon," by D.H. Lawrence.

Susan might wander in the moon or, as cows will, jump over it, yet the meaning of her conduct would escape all but children or adepts. To the latter, especially to theosophists, cow and moon and their almost unspeakable connection are known; for the wisdom of the East, handed down from Atlantis and preserved by Hindus, Chaldeans, Egyptians, and Mme Blavatsky, has unveiled the theosophical eye by which the truth is perceived. Through this eye, William Butler Yeats contemplated cats and the eight-and-twenty phases of the moon; and D.H. Lawrence saw Susan plain in the loony night.

From *D.H. Lawrence & Susan His Cow,* by William Tindall.

... They managed to get the running water working, to irrigate the field; and that early in June, they acquired chickens (which Frieda cared for) and a cow, Susan, Lawrence's responsibility. This saved them the daily journeys for milk down to Del Monte ... though Lawrence then had to spend an inordinate amount of time chasing his cow, to milk her. (Susan would run away if he showed up wearing pants she did not like.)

"We've just sat tight and considered the lily all summer," (Lawrence wrote in letter V: 291) ... "the only excitements being the perpetual looking for Susan ... "

From *The Biography of D.H. Lawrence,* by John Worthen.

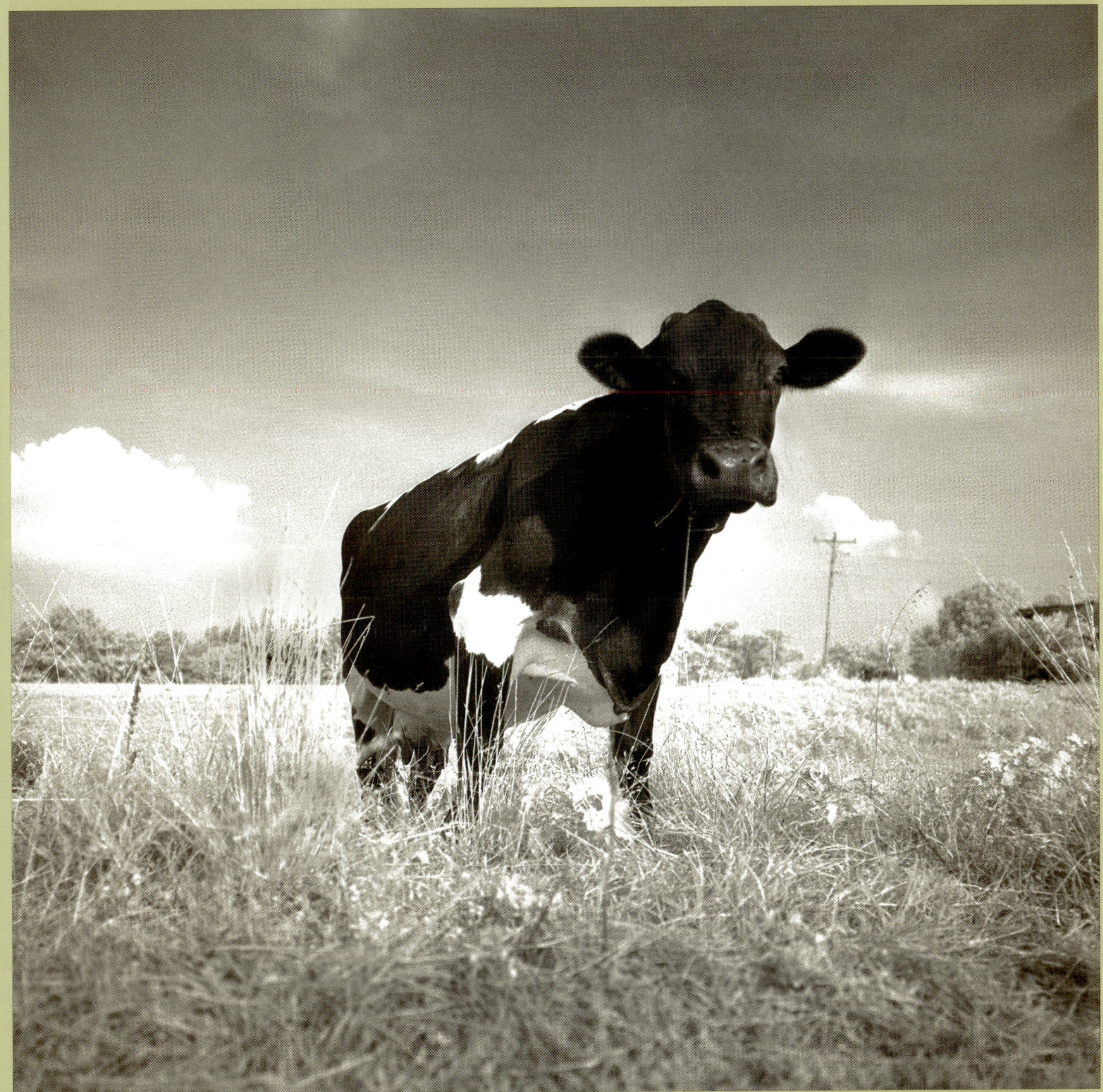

The Vanity of Cows

STATE FAIR HAS A COW ABOUT BOVINE HAIRPIECES

COLUMBUS, Ohio (AP)—Three livestock exhibitors at last year's Ohio State Fair have been disqualified for allegedly outfitting their Holstein cows with hairpieces. State Fair inspectors said the three glued or painted hair from another part of the animal or from another animal to create straighter backs on the cows and enhance their appearance in the show ring. Kreg Krebs and his brother Kenneth of Fredericksburg, and Scott Long of Clayton, Michigan, could be required to forfeit all winnings, said Department of Agriculture spokeswoman Melanie Wilt. The winnings had been withheld by fair officials. Wilt said state inspectors at the fair discovered the fake hair when the cows were leaving the show ring on Aug. 10th.

Associated Press Story.

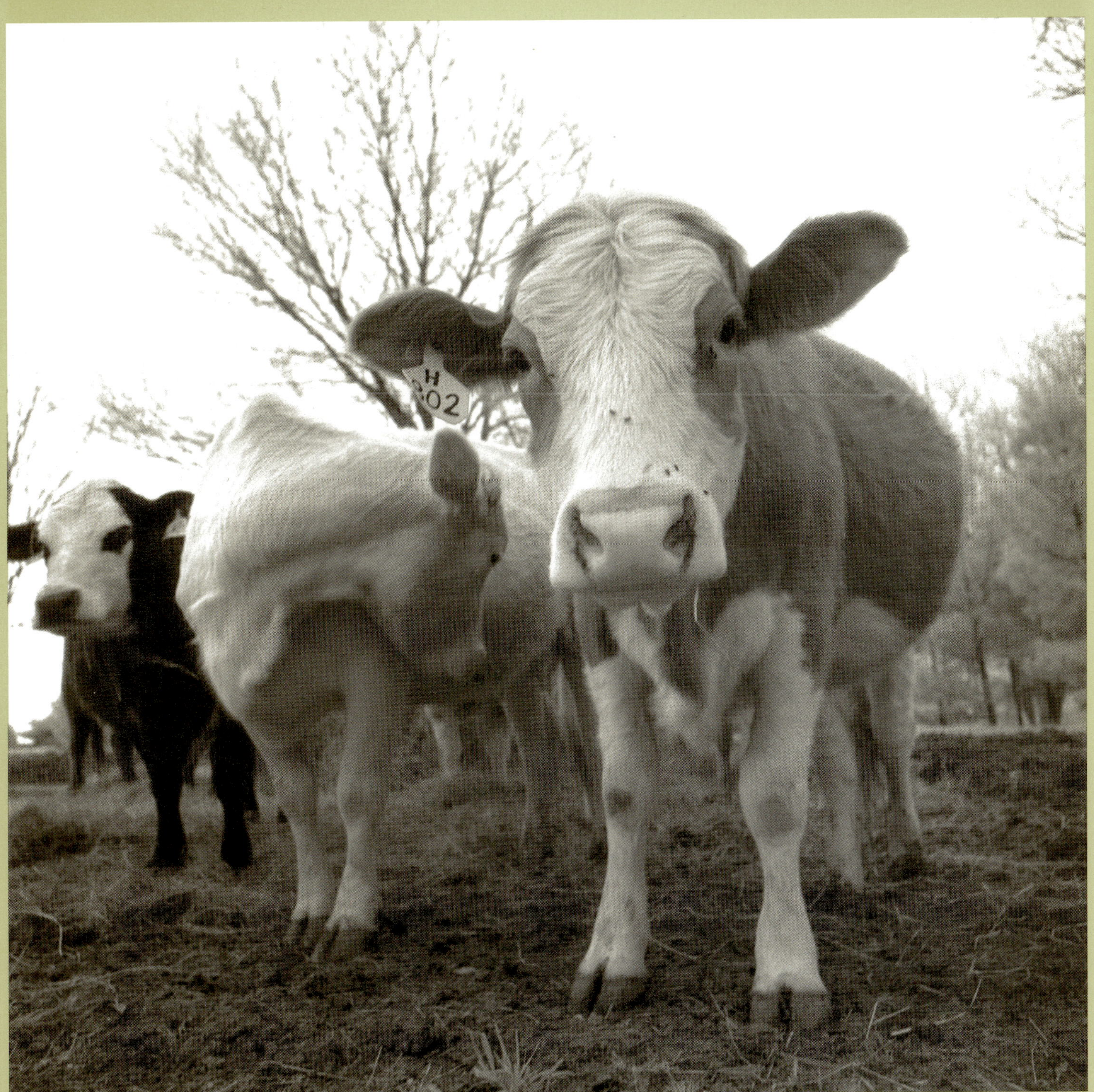
H

The Misfortune of Cows

by Paul Sylbert

I worked on one western in my career as a film production designer. It was in the Flint Hills of Kansas. There was no cattle drive, no struggles between ranchers and farmers, but there *was* a stagecoach, and plenty of shooting. I had already seen to the building of a sod house and some very scrappy outbuildings. I added a lone cow, which symbolized for me the isolation of the West and rural innocence.

The morning of the shoot I arrived to find the cameraman standing on the road above the valley in which the set stood. He looked miserable, his woolen cap pulled low over his brow.

"BLANK wants to remove those extra buildings," he said, referring to the director, who shall remain nameless.

I looked down at the set and saw a group huddled near the sod house. Among the gathered heads I noticed the director.

"Why doesn't he ask me himself?"

"He asked me to ask you."

This film was the director's solo flight. I had taken it on as a favor to the producer, and I considered the director's request an impertinence. But I did, and still do, believe that experience trumps vision anytime. So I walked down to the construction crew, which was standing near the outbuildings and also looking miserable.

"Strike the stuff carefully," I told them, "and lay it over there." I pointed to some tall grass about twenty feet away. The crew quickly dismantled the outbuildings. Since the director hadn't thought it necessary to talk to me, I didn't bother to talk to him. I did point to the lone cow and got a negative headshake from the cameraman.

I climbed the hill again, got into my car and tore back to my office. Less than an hour later I got a call from the set informing me that the director wanted the outbuildings back up. I didn't bother to act surprised. I told the construction coordinator to do as the director wanted. Then I asked about the cow. "It went back to the feedlot," he said. I realized this meant that the cow was likely on her way to the slaughterhouse. I said, "What a shame," and hung up.

There is justice, however, even in the world of film: The movie lasted longer than the cow, but not by much.

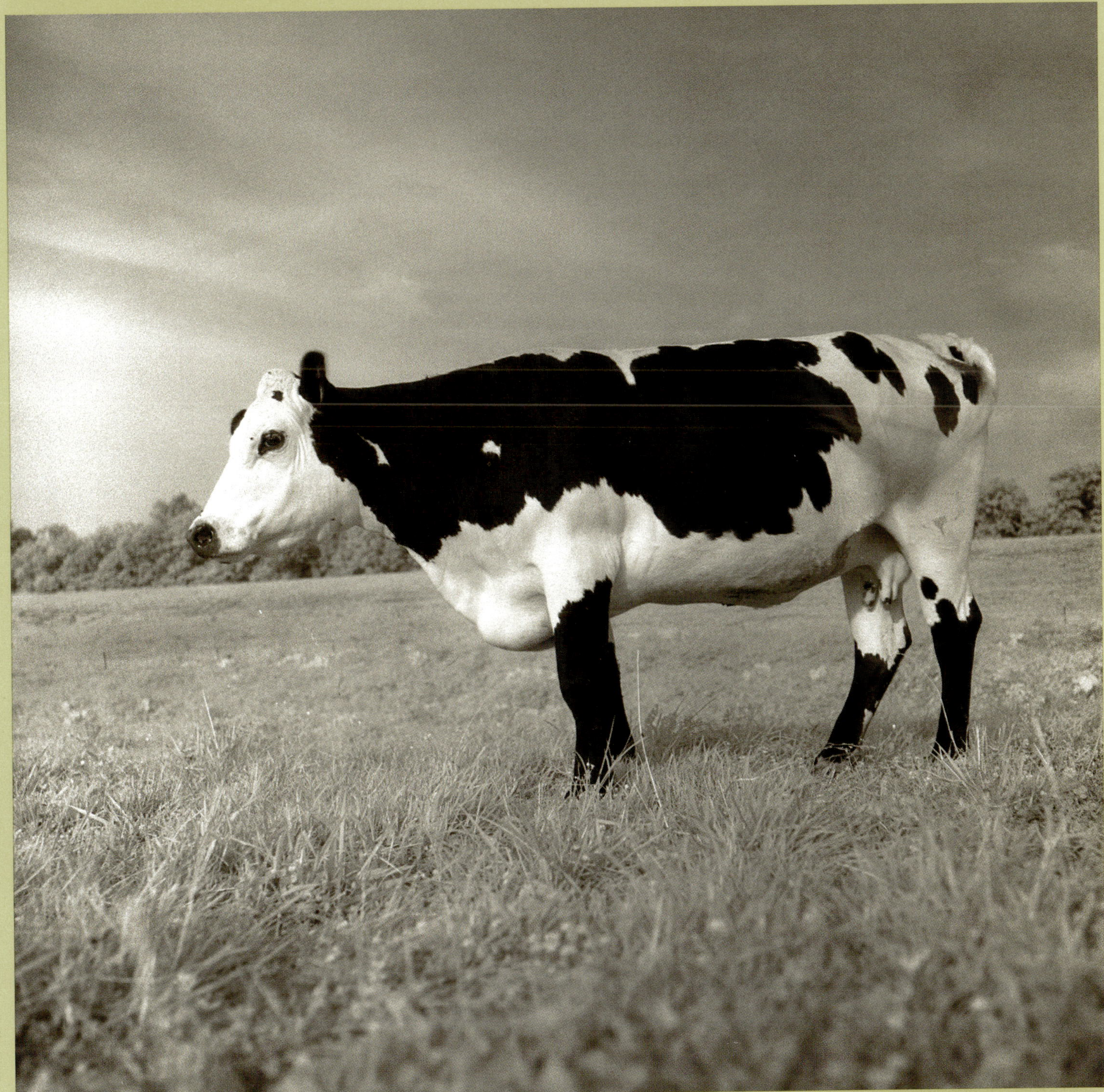

The Neccessity of Cows

Milk Cow Blues

Well, I woke up this morning,
And I looked out the door.
I can tell that old milk cow
By the way she lowed.
Well, if you've seen my milk cow,
Please ride her on home.
I ain't had no milk or butter
Since that cow's been gone.

—Song Lyrics by Sleepy John Estes

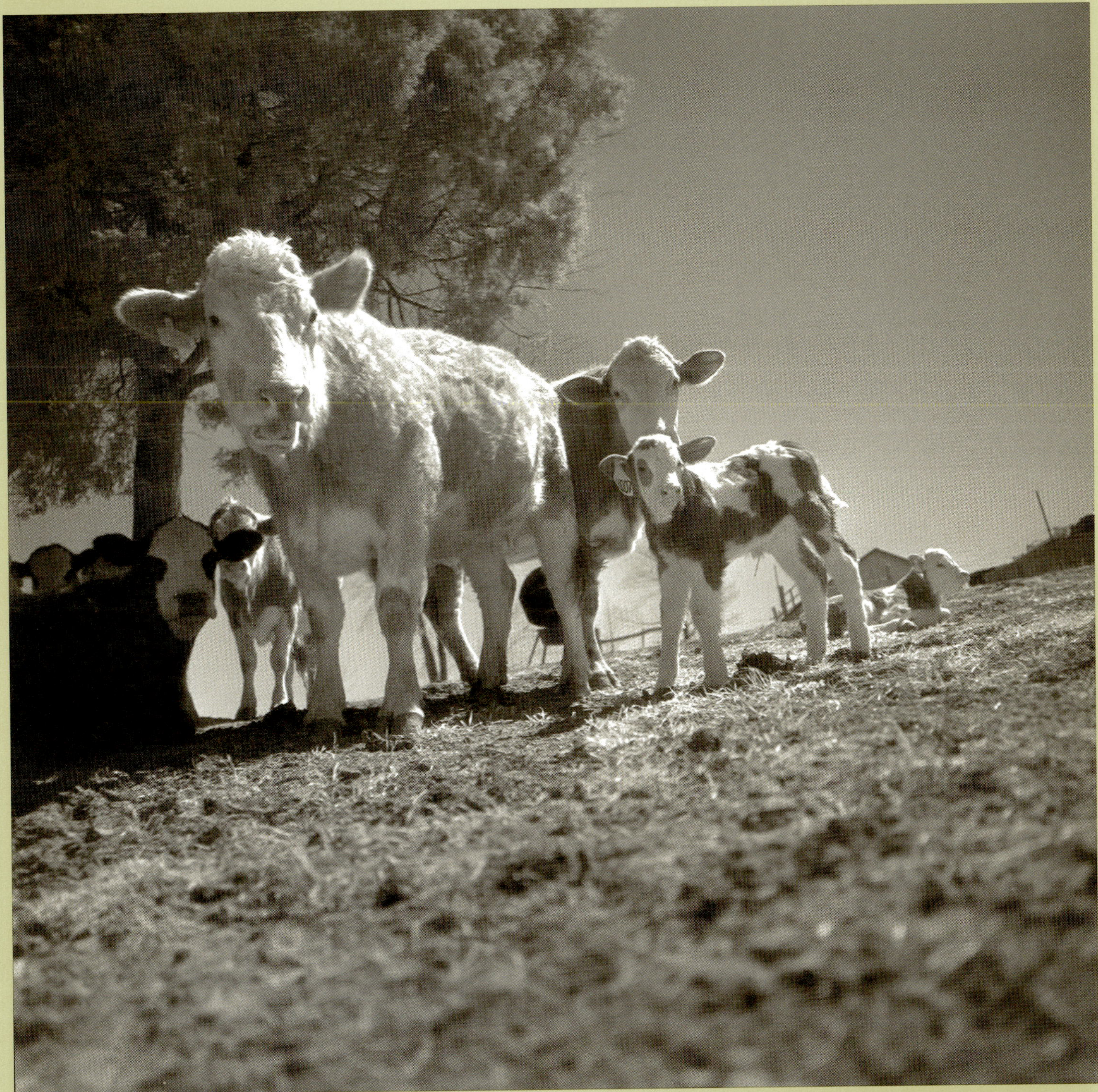

The Addiction of Cows

by Dr. Paul Gahlinger

MILK FROM CONTENTED COWS read the enormous sign at Borden's dairy. Each day when I was a child, I would pass that sign on the school bus from our farm to town, and think, "Is that so?"

My father was a dairy farmer, as was his father, back in Switzerland, and his father, and so on for at least five hundred years according to the church records. I have no doubt that my ice-age ancestors milked the family aurochs while grilling steaks of its less compliant Pleistocene siblings. So I came to know the quirks of cows, including that dopey spaced-out contentment of one that has fed where it shouldn't.

Cows are not among the most intelligent of creatures, but then neither are those of our own species who become alcoholics or drug addicts. It doesn't take much. A cow that has munched a few fermenting berries will seek out more, and more, until it can barely stumble and lies down, wheezing and farting in a slobbering stupefaction. Cannabis is a particular treat for the cow lucky enough to come across it, and once savored it is never forgotten. Wild tobacco is another delight to a bored cow. And a ton of meat on the hoof hallucinating from psilocybin mushrooms is a sight to behold—bellowing at imaginary snakes and blundering into surprisingly real fences. And yet they go back for more. Indeed, the best place to look for psilocybin is in cow patties, from spores that have survived the bovine intestinal journey.

Like its owner, a drunk or stoned cow evokes humor or disgust. But the hard addict is no joke. The word alone strikes fear into the dairyman. Locoweed. After an initial nibble, a cow will begin to seek it out, ignoring normal feed even to the point of starvation. Just like a human addict, the loco eater wastes away. The normally sociable animal becomes a loner, freakish, stiff-legged and twitchy, rousing itself only to look for more locoweed.

Can we fault the gentle cow for wanting to get high? So udderly productive and so utterly bored. Those huge brown eyes may hide the secret of a silly contentment.

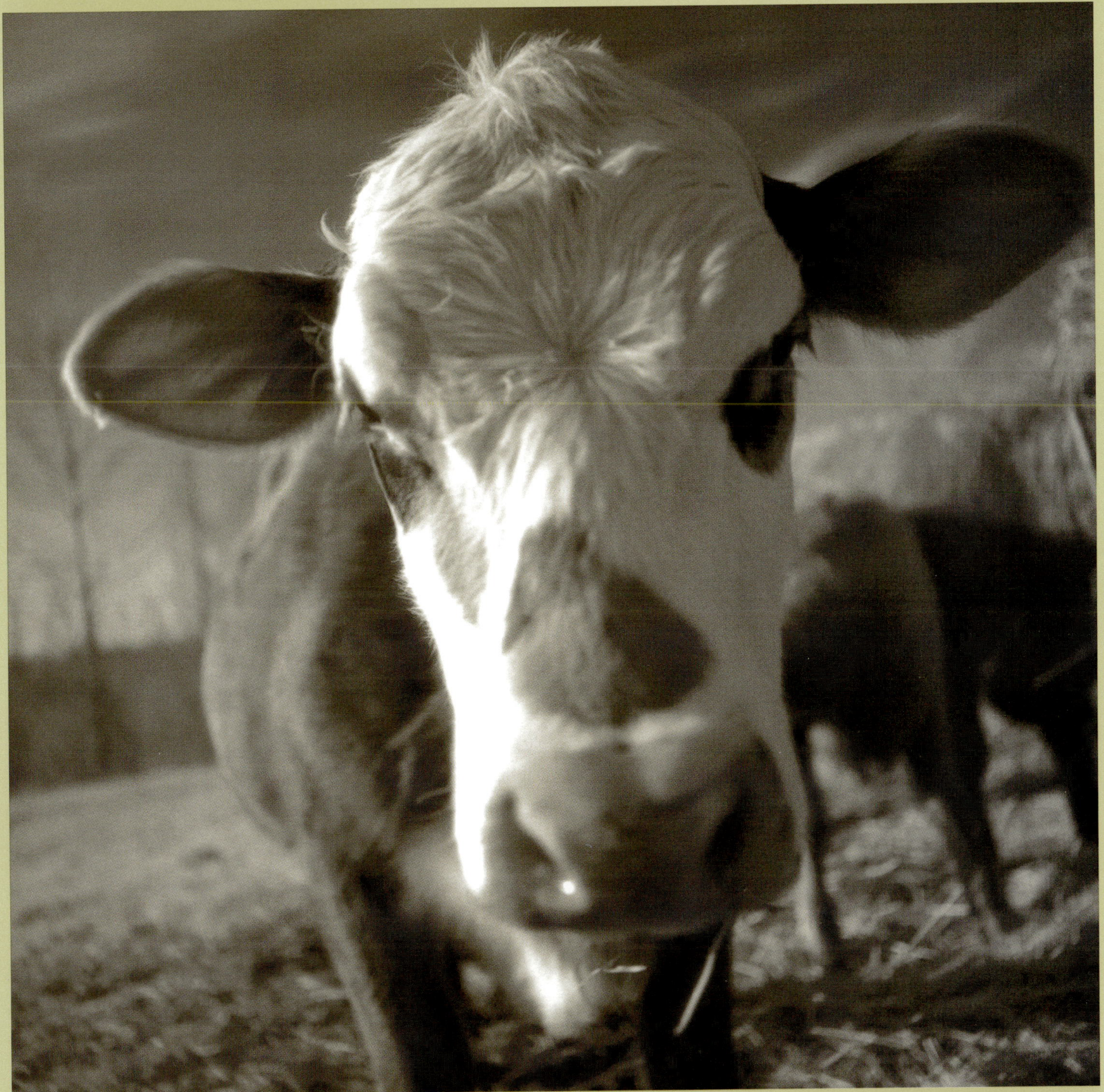

The Genetics of Cows

In a communist system, according to the list that's been circulating forever on the Internet, "You have two cows. The government takes both cows and gives you the milk." Fidel Castro has a new twist on this. Today's *Wall Street Journal* reports that the Cubans want to clone Ubre Blanca, a record-setting cow that once produced 241 pounds of milk in a single day. The cow died in 1985, but Cuban scientists preserved its eggs.

The *Journal* reports:

Building a better cow has long been an obsession of Mr. Castro's. In a 1987 speech, he said super cows could be achieved under a socialist system, where scientists and the government both pull in the same direction. "If another Ubre Blanca is found or a prodigious descendant of Ubre Blanca capable of producing cows giving 100 quarts a day, what can prevent us from immediately applying that practice ... to all the cows of the country?" he asked.

That same year, Mr. Castro proposed his scientists shrink cows to the size of dogs, says Boris Luis Garcia, a molecular biologist who worked for three years at the Center for Genetic Engineering and Biotechnology. The idea: solve the scarcity of milk in the cities by providing families with miniature milk-cows they could keep in their apartments.

The pint-sized beasts would graze on grass grown in drawers under fluorescent lights. "That was what Castro had planned for us," says Mr. Garcia, who now lives in Spain. Nothing ever came of it.

James Taranto, Editor, *OpinionJournal.com*

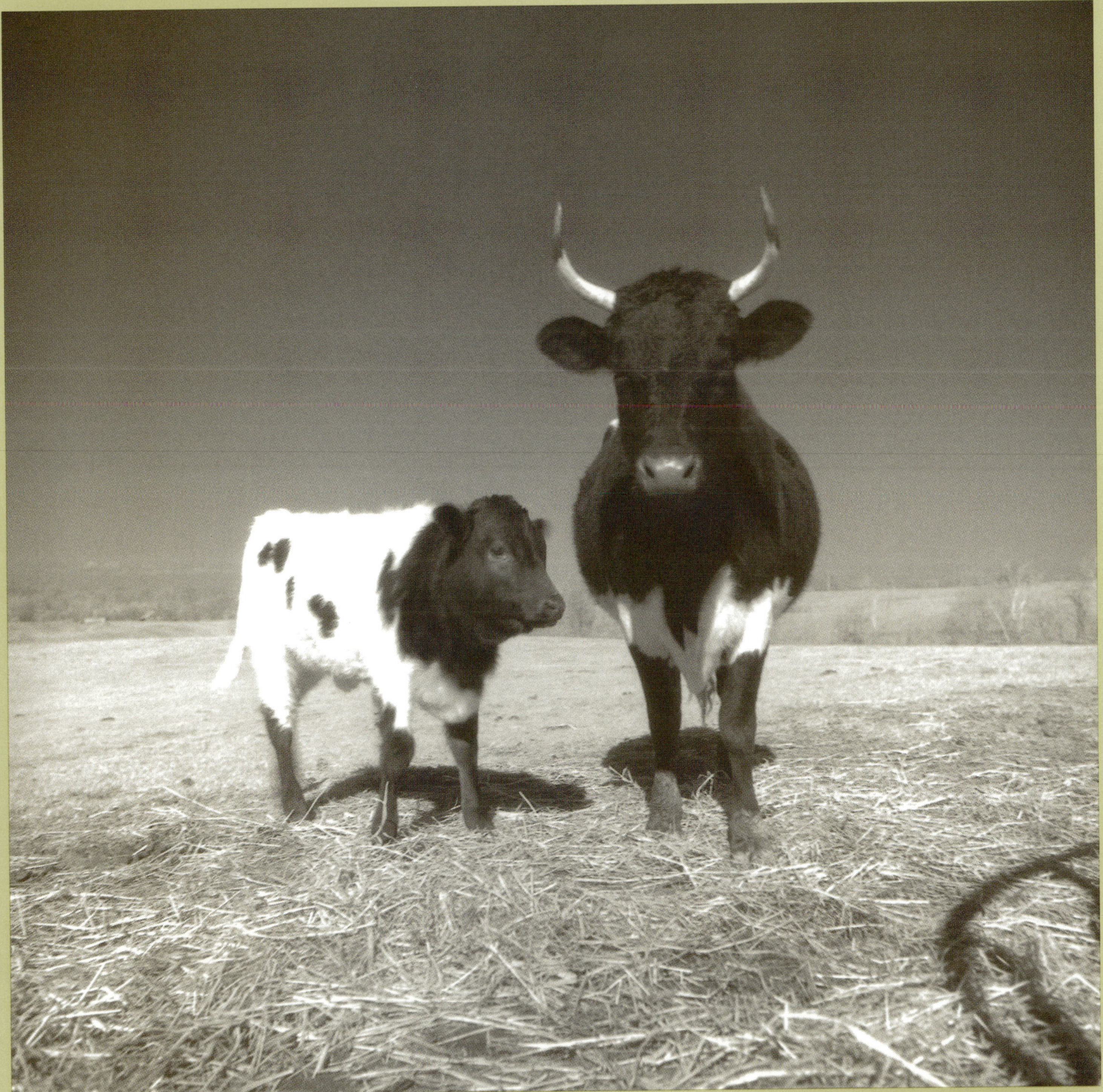

The Miracle of Cows

by Bill Brown

My grandmother told this story to my sister and me when we were children. We spent part of each summer on my grandparents' farm in Bible Hills, Tennessee. The narrator is the imagined voice of my father, who was a boy in the occasion of the poem. My grandfather was a short, quiet man who was powerful both in heart and in physical strength. He was known in the river bluff counties for being a healer of people and animals. He rode his horse around the farm talking to his cows by name. Most started with the letter M: Millie, Matilda, Mary, Martha, Melissa, May. My father, who died when I was sixteen, never commented on the validity of the story. I like to think it's true.

That Morning

That morning in the dark
I tripped on frozen hoof prints
all the way toward the blaring bulb
hanging in the barn,
and rubbing sleep from my eyes,
saw the birth-wet calf
my father saved.
With her eyes wide open despite the glare,
the mother licked its matted fur,
still steaming from the cold.
We smelled breakfast before it was ready
and long before we were ready to eat.
My father couldn't take his eyes
off the calf. Staring in disbelief,
he told me about his night dream
of being upside down in Wolf River Cave,
how his feet and shoulders seemed
bound in the opposite direction,
and struggling, he awakened mother,
and she shook him up.
It was then that he heard
Melissa lowing in the pasture.
When he got there with a light
all he could see was the back
of a calf, stuck.
He reached his hand in deep
to find its head and turned
the calf around in the mother's well,
all the time wondering if he
had broken its neck,
and then she dropped it in
his lap like a present.
It was a story that had to be told
before he washed the caked blood
from his hands and signaled for breakfast.

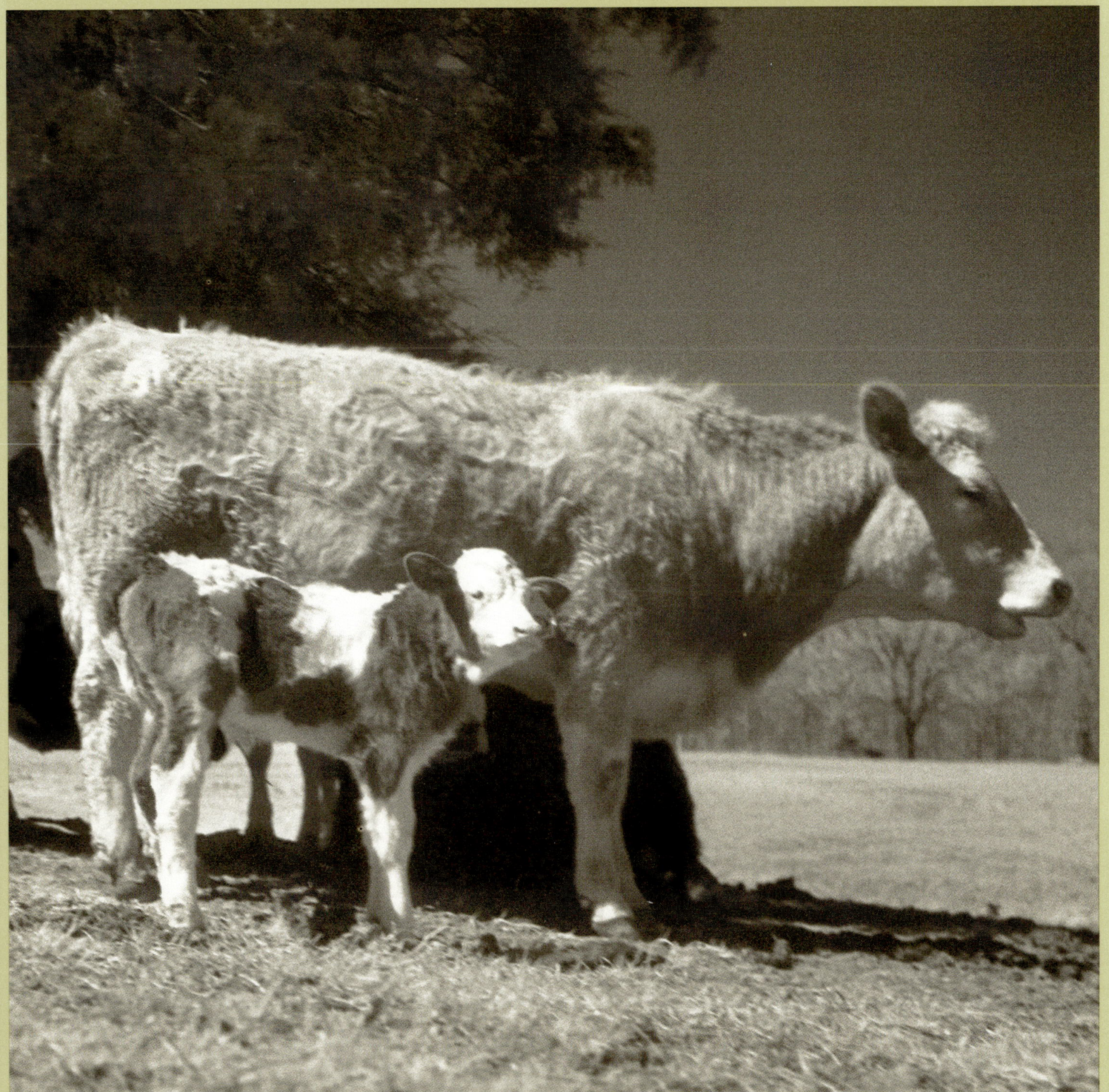

The Truth of Cows

Truth, Sir, is a cow which will yield skeptics no more milk,
and so they are gone to milk the bull.

—Samuel Johnson

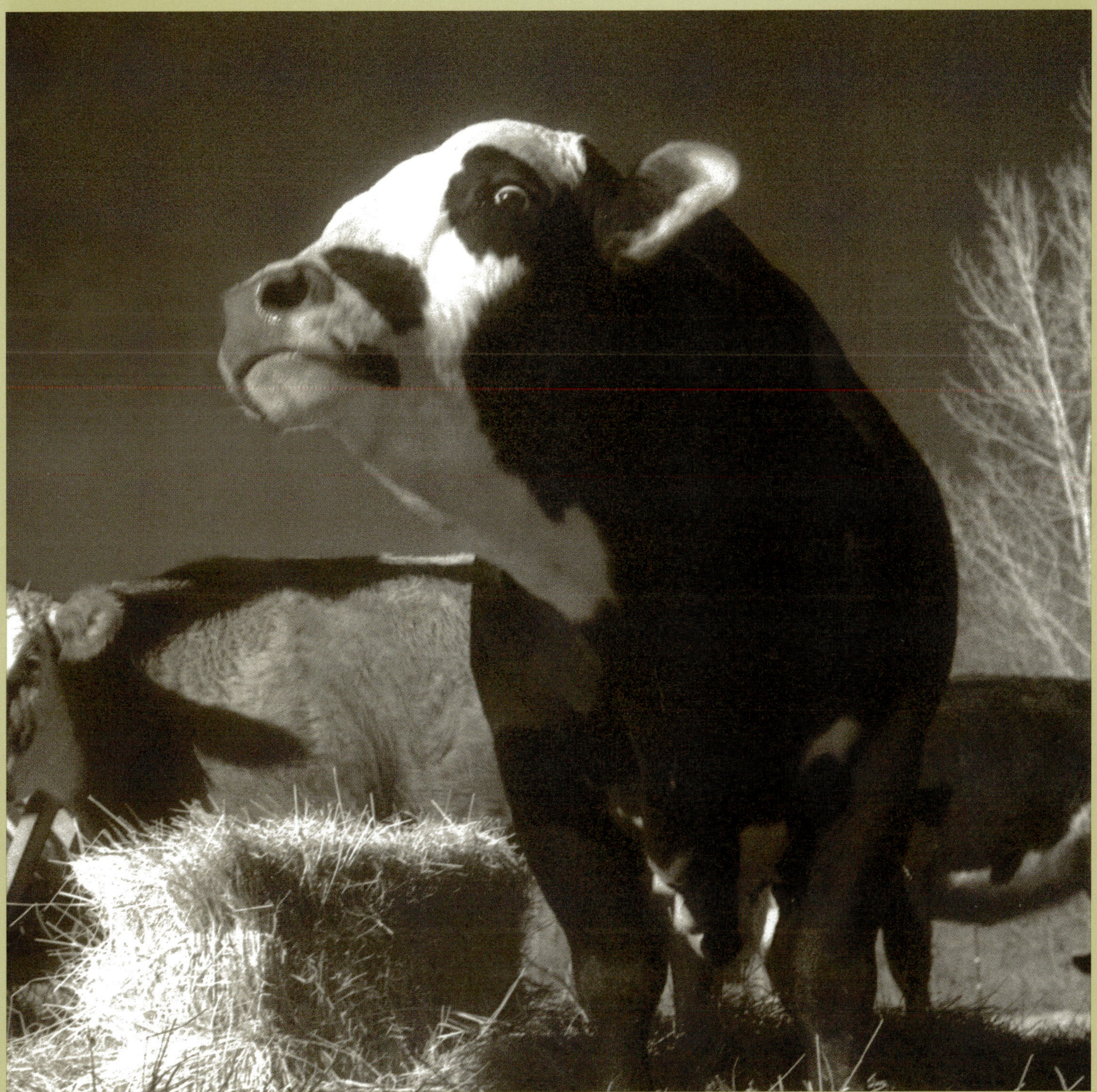

The Parable of Cows

by Larry Gatlin

My son, Josh, is a fine young man who believes in right and wrong. He believes there are goalposts in the game of life, and that those posts don't move. He knows, of course, that no one kicks the ball through the goalposts every time, but believes we should all at least strive to do so, instead of moving the goalposts to accommodate any wayward kicks of the ball.

Much of Josh's world view stems from his upbringing by his saintly mother, Janis, who reared our kids (you *rear* children, you *raise* corn) according to the guidelines set down in the Good Book. But in addition to that teaching, Josh got some first-hand experience at this thing called *life* on our ninety-acre farm.

One day when Josh was about four years old, he and I were walking out in the "big field" on the far side of the barn. Across the fence, in my neighbor's field, some "bovine activity" was going on. A big red bull was servicing a small black-and-white cow. Josh stopped walking and stood, quietly transfixed, staring at this romantic interlude.

"Josh, what do you think is going on over there on Miss Jenny's farm?" I asked.

"Well," he answered, "I think the red one is tryin' to help the black-and-white one over the fence."

I had to stifle a laugh. When I regained my composure, I said, "I think you're right. We could learn a lesson from those animals. When a neighbor needs help, we should always be available to lend a hand ... or *whatever*!"

"That's right," he said. "We should always help our neighbors and even people we don't know." How could I not be a proud father?

Twenty-four years have passed since that day. Now and then, I find myself reflecting on the humorous and yet wonderful comments exchanged between father and son. And so, I offer this up as my own view of the world, that maybe it would be a better place if there were more people like Josh. And such a world would arrive *post haste* if we would all try to help our neighbor over the fence, instead of trying to screw everybody at every opportunity.

Maybe it's time for some "Good Book-Farm Boy Philosophy!"

Keep the faith.

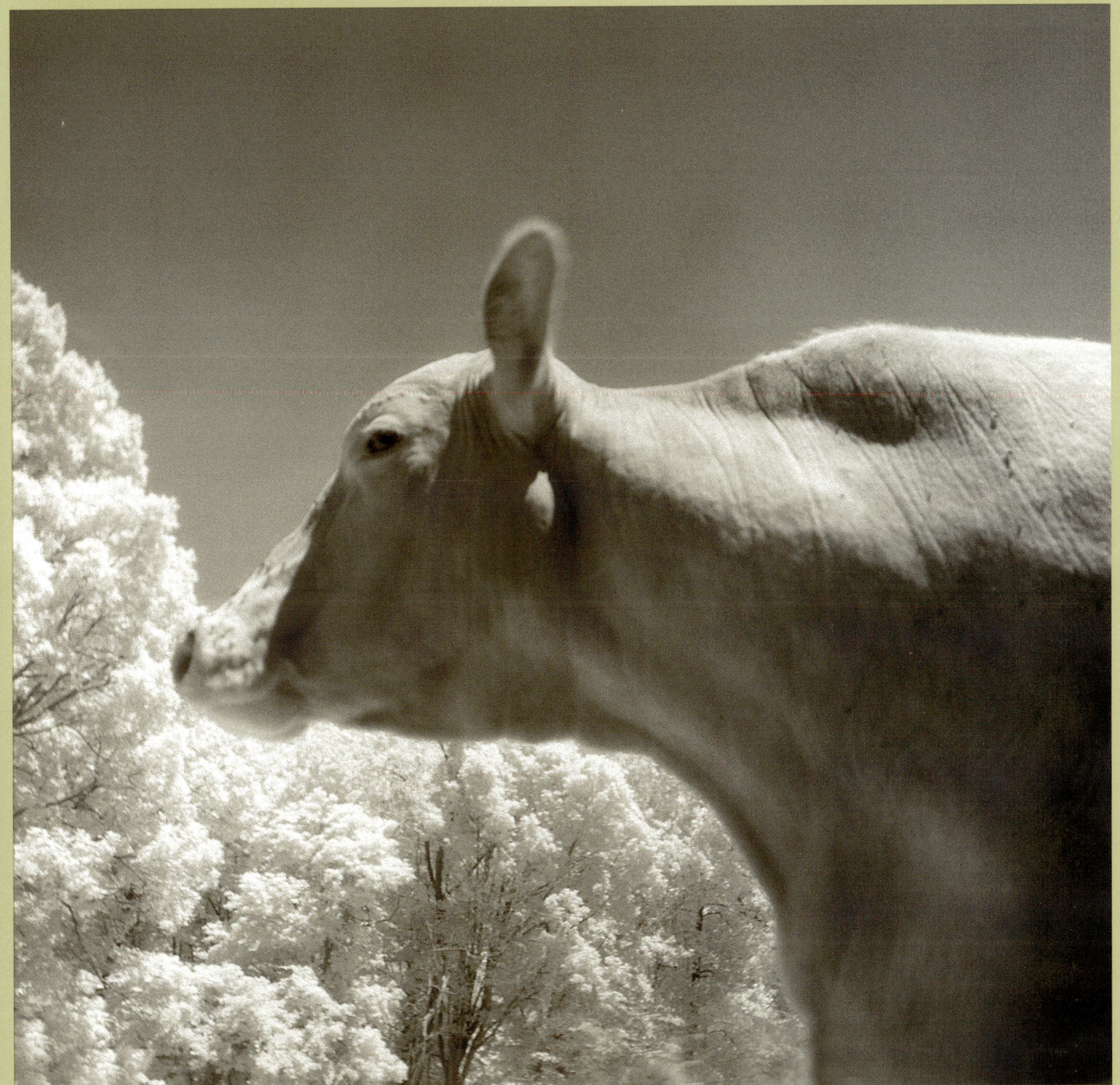

The Acceptance of Cows

by Mike Kimball

One fine day some years back I used all of my carpentry skills to convert a long boat trailer into a long wooden junk-hauling trailer to transport my trash to the dump. On its maiden voyage, the trailer broke free of the car. I watched in my mirror as the thing came fishtailing and sparking after me. Then, suddenly, it catapulted into this amazing double-twisting trailer routine that actually began disassembling before it flattened the cow fence and crashed in the pasture. When all was finally quiet, the area looked as if some kind of primitive flying machine had fallen out of the sky. Debris? Holy friggin' catfish! Then I noticed the cows. The commotion had brought them all ambling up from the farthest corners of the passage. Did they make a break through the hole in the fence? Nope. They gathered around me in a polite little circle and watched while I cleaned up my mess. I wondered if they suspected that I had made a mistake. I didn't let on that I had.

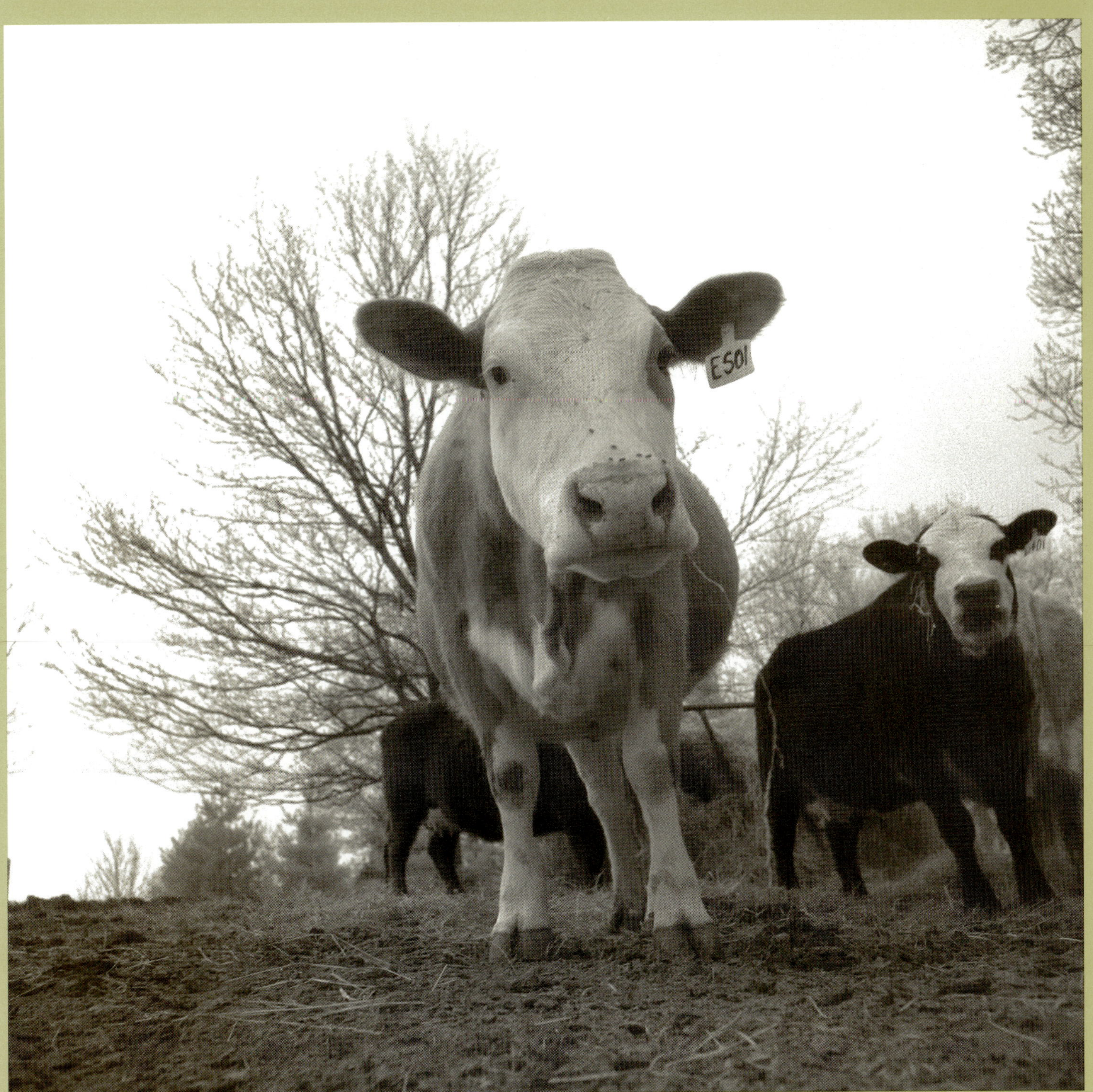
E501

The Escapade of Cows

by Flora Strong Farmer

In 1910, when I was eight years old, Pleas Isaacs' son, Robert, tied his wrist to a cow's tail and created a lot of excitement in our community. Living in the foothills of the Appalachian Mountains of Kentucky, we were not prone to witnessing exciting events. We had seen Halley's Comet that same year, but no one knew what it was. People could only conjecture about the fiery star with a tail that lit up the sky. It was not until the *Louisville Courier-Journal* arrived a week later that we knew what we'd seen. But Robert Isaac's escapade was more memorable than any comet.

One of Mrs. Isaac's chores was to milk the cow. On this eventful day she took Robert to the barn with her so he could bring the cow up from the pasture. It was a warm summer evening and flies were buzzing around the cow, causing her to swat them with her tail. This swatting made it difficult for Mrs. Isaacs to do the milking. "Hold that cow's tail," she told Robert, and that's when he took hold of the tail. Now, why he decided to take the long hair at the end of the tail and tie it to his wrist has never been satisfactorily explained. But that's what he did. From this point on, events happened fast and furious. When the cow tried to swat flies and realized that her tail had lost its mobility, she panicked and wheeled around. This threw Robert against his mother, knocking her from the stool. The cow then decided that the best place to be was away from the barn. Robert had already lowered two of the fence rails, and now the cow removed the rest with the shins of the boy, who was trying desperately to free himself.

All Mrs. Pleas could see, from her position on the barn floor, was what appeared to be her son chasing the cow. "Robert," she yelled, "bring that cow back this instant!" Pleas Isaacs, sitting on his front porch, heard the commotion. When he saw his son, who seemed to be deviling the cow by holding its tail, he yelled, "Robert, turn that darn cow loose!" By this time, the whole community was involved, either chasing Robert and the cow, or as enthusiastic spectators.

It was at this point in the chase across the pasture that Robert fell. The cow then dragged him through the briar patch. The episode ended only when the cow ran out of breath and Pleas cut the boy loose with a pocket knife. Fortunately, Robert suffered little harm, but the cow did not recover as rapidly. She refused to give milk for an indefinite time.

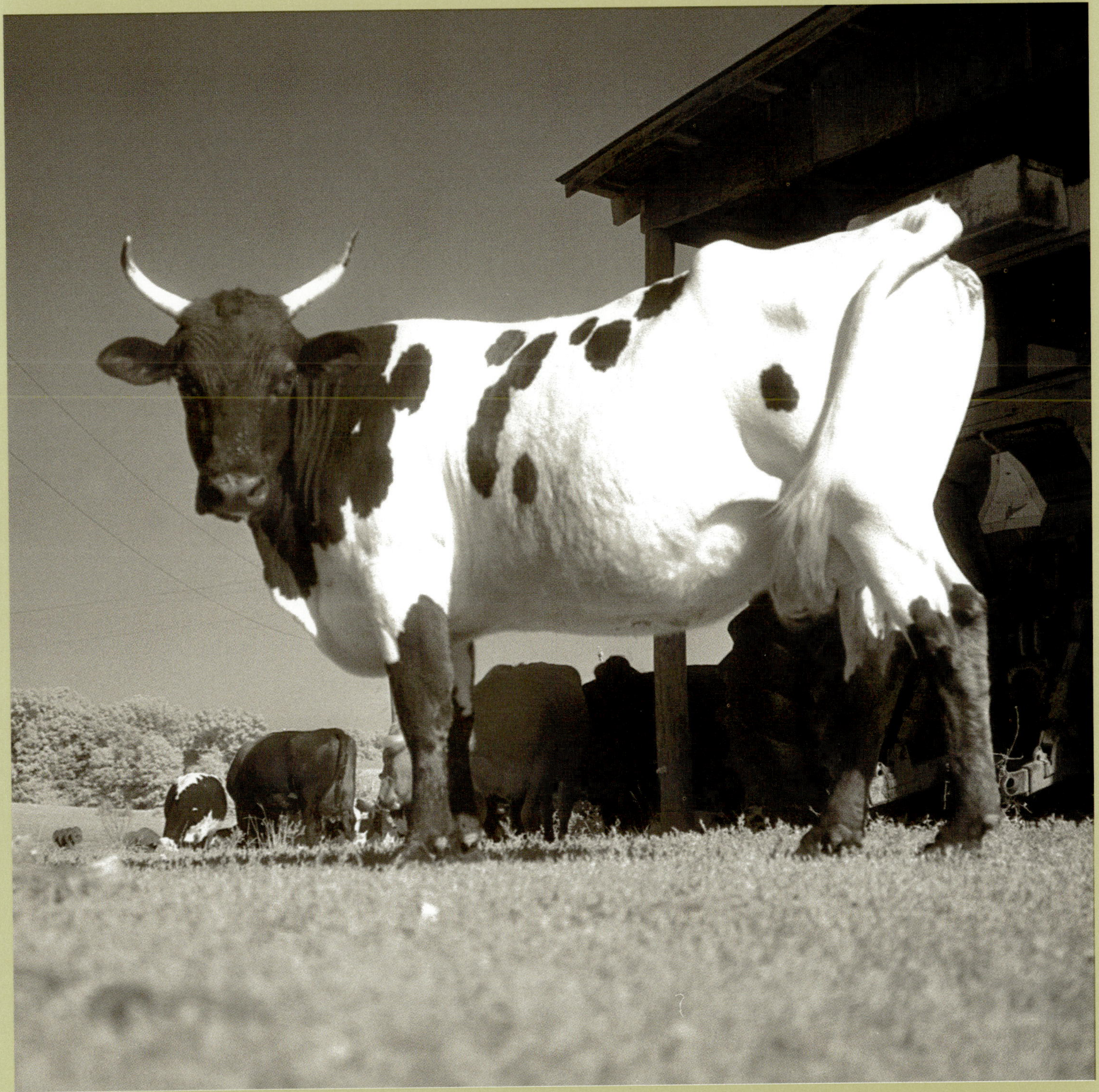

The Love of Cows

by Erica Johnson

What makes me happy? COWS!

I live on a dairy farm, and cows are basically my whole entire life. I see them every day, and I milk them every night with my dad. One of our oldest cows is Olivia, and she's eight years old, which is very old in cow years. She's one of my favorites because she listens to your problems and never tells anyone. One of my other favorite cows is Clover. She's not even two years old yet.

I sleep with the cows all the time. They don't even move or care, and then I fall asleep. When I wake up, they're still laying down like they know not to hurt me.

My happiest moment was when I got to see a calf being born.

THAT was very cool!

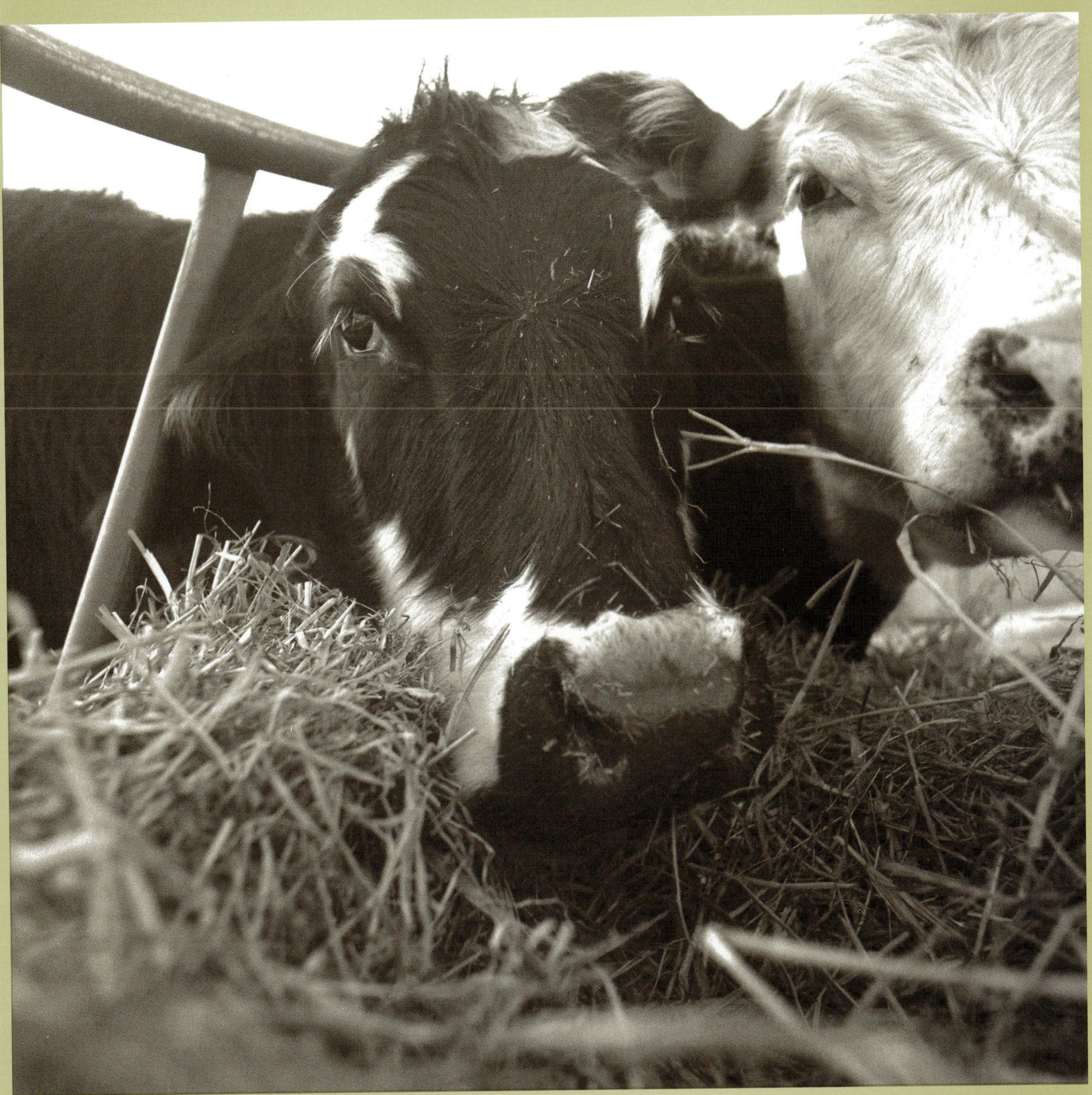

The Bacchanalia of Cows

The Cow in Apple-Time

Something inspires the only cow of late
To make no more of a wall than an open gate,
And think no more of wall-builders than fools.
Her face is flecked with pomace and she drools
A cider syrup. Having tasted fruit,
She scorns a pasture withering to the root.
She runs from tree to tree where lie and sweeten.
The windfalls spiked with stubble and worm-eaten.
She leaves them bitten when she has to fly.
She bellows on a knoll against the sky.
Her udder shrivels and the milk goes dry.

—Robert Frost

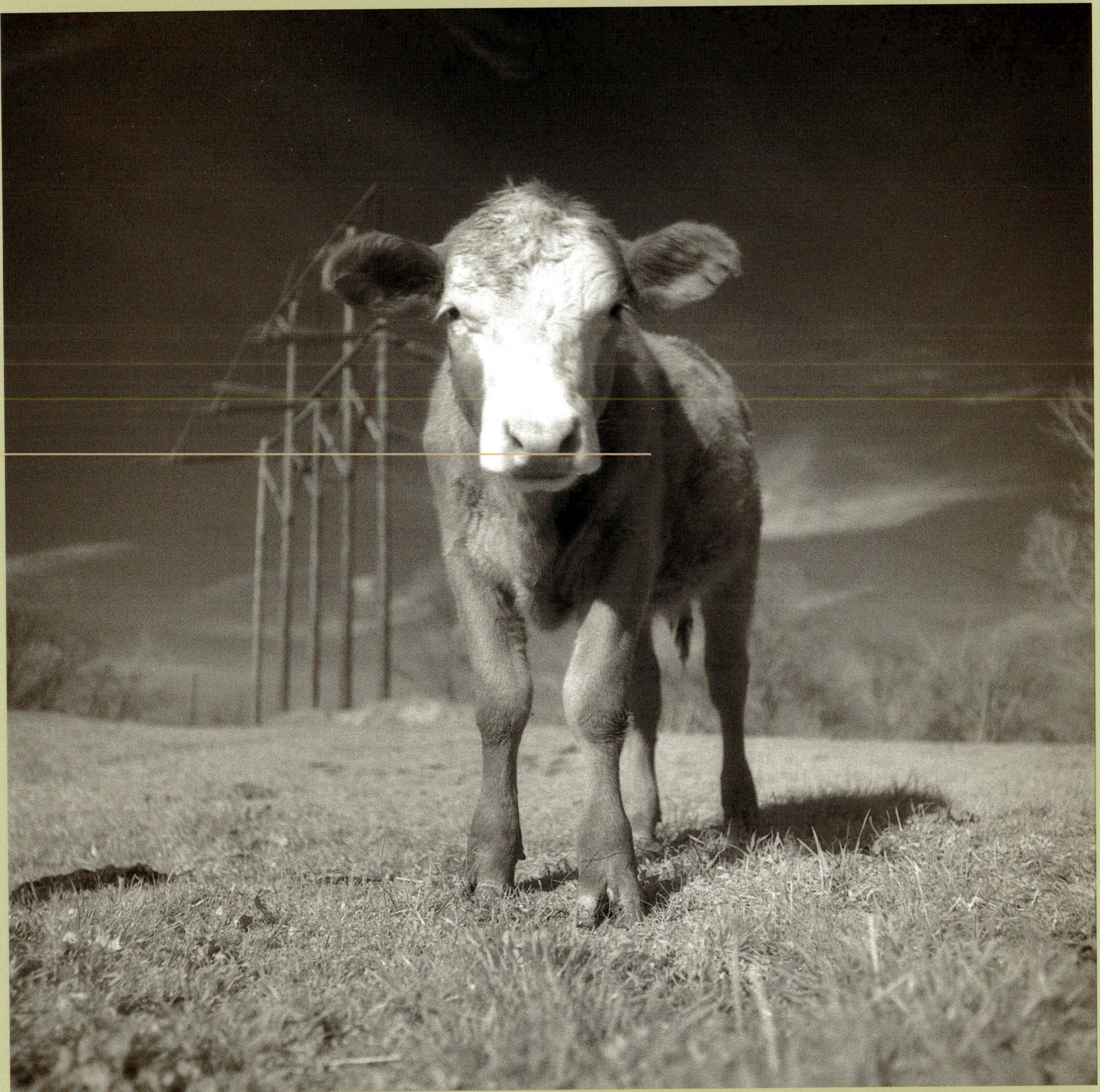

The Usefulness of Cows

The following is a list of products, foods, and medicines we get directly from cows, or from the manufacture of cow by-products: Crayons, upholstery, floor wax, detergents, plastics, cosmetics, paints, violin strings, glue, fabric softeners, shaving cream, shampoo, cream rinses, boots, shoes, insecticides, toothpaste, textiles, soaps, deodorants, candles, luggage, bone china, doggie chews, bone meal biscuits, pet food, hydraulic brake fluid, asphalt, airplane production, steel ball bearings containing bone charcoal, antifreeze, car tires, whitener for paper, cement blocks, printing ink, high gloss for magazines, fertilizers, industrial cleaners, dry wall, marshmallows, ice cream, chewing gum, cookies, sausage casings, oleo shortening, mayonnaise, yogurt, gelatin clarification agent for juices, wines and beer, beef cheese, milk, Insulin used in the treatment of diabetes, pancreatin used in the treatment of infants with celiac diseases, heparin used in the treatment of rheumatoid arthritis and respiratory diseases, fibrinolysin used to prevent blood clots within the cardiovascular system, thrombin for promoting coagulation during surgery, trypsin used to clean wounds, glucagon used in the treatment of hypoglycemia, sodium levathroxine used in thyroid replacement therapy, collagen used in cosmetic surgery, and albumin used in cancer research.

Therefore, the next time you wax your car, brush your teeth, print pages from your computer, or buy film for your camera, you might think that we humans are very clever to have invented those wonderful items. But think again. Or better yet, perhaps you might *ruminate* on the subject. The success we've made during our short time on the planet hasn't been just about humans. It's also been about cows.

From *About Cows,* artist's statement, from the photographic exhibition by Carl Hileman.

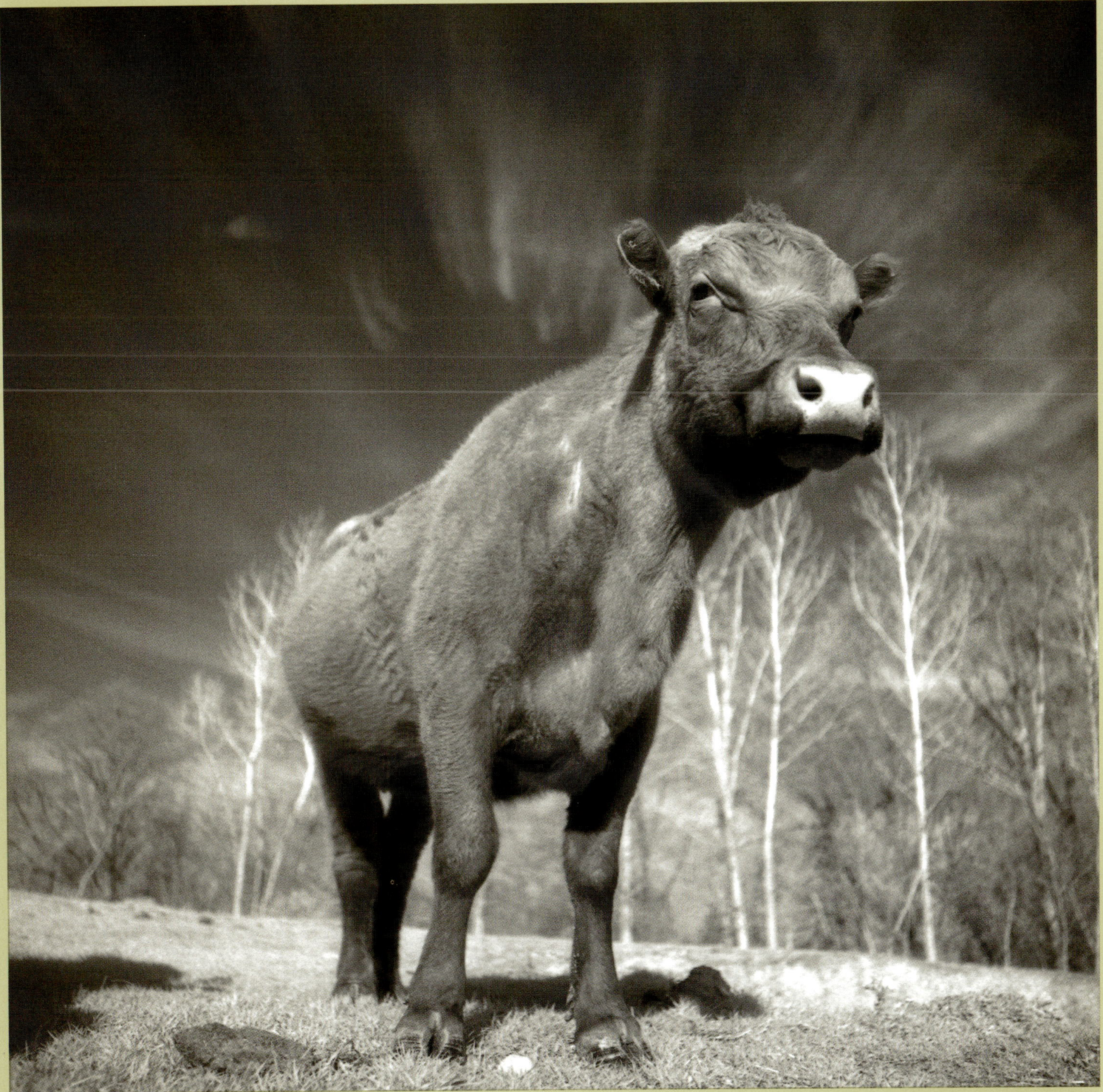

The Rhythm of Cows

"I could dance with you till the cows come home.
Better still, I'll dance with the cows until you come home."

—Groucho Marx, *Duck Soup*

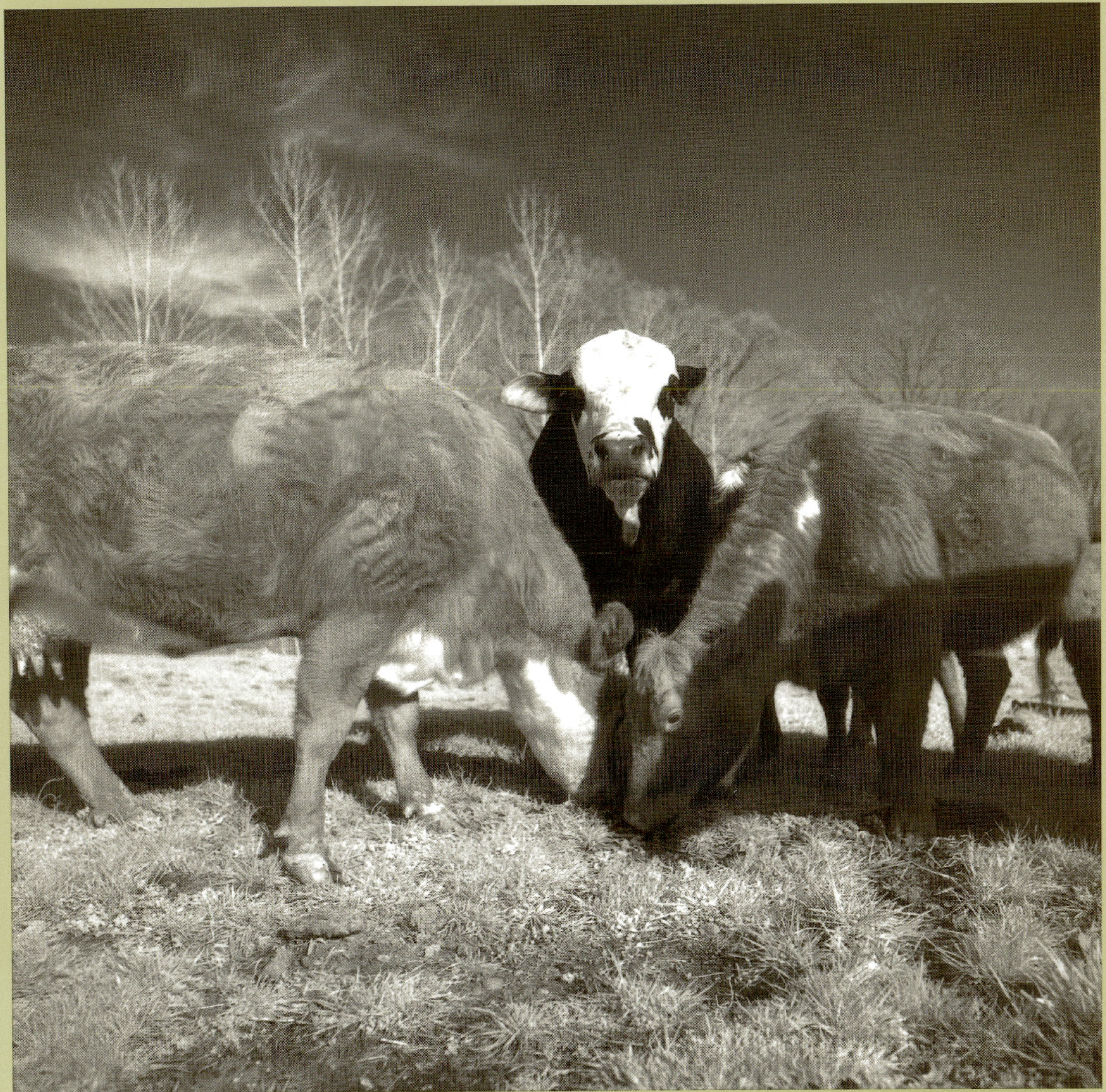

The Future Cow

by Jeffrey A. Carver

Age five, maybe six. Thanksgiving at Grandma and Grandpa's farm in Wooster, Ohio. I especially loved wandering down to the barn. Looking for kittens, smelling the hay. Hanging over the animal-pen railings, hoping to touch the cows hunkered and puffing in the cold. Who would have thought one of them would give me another cowlick?

(I *hated* the dopey cowlick I'd always had over my forehead. My *brother* didn't have a dumb cowlick, why should I?)

Dunno what I was thinking about as I leaned back against the worn wooden railing, encased in my snowsuit. Probably wondering where all the cats had gone.

Whump. A soft blow to the head. I yelled in annoyance, thinking one of my cousins had hit me. "The cow did it!" someone said, giggling. I turned, indignant. Gazing mournfully back at me was the cow that had just licked me on the back of the head.

Licked me? *Licked me?*

Heaven knows what my cousins thought as I ran crying up to the house. *I just got licked by a cow! Now I've got another cowlick!* Never mind what they thought, anyway. I was right. Sure enough, checking with my mom and grandma, I found I had not just one cowlick, but two. The second was right on the crown of my head, where the cow licked me. Coincidence? No way.

Nowadays I write stories set in the future, and this has got me to wondering what the future holds for cows. I like to think this one had a little fun at my expense, and whether that's true or not, I still somehow feel a connection to the lumbering beasts—the invisible herds out there at the other end of the milk pipeline as well as the ones whose eyes I have looked into. I wonder if in the future we will *allow* cows to be cows, playful and imaginative or not. Or will we reduce them to bulky containers of useful protoplasm, dumb machines inputting feed and outputting milk? Or will we even let them be that? Will we have vats of cow-derived gray goo, nanotechnologically producing Enhanced Milk at a thousand times the efficiency of the real thing?

I hope not. I've never put any cows into my stories, but maybe I should. As a kind of talisman against the market forces that would do that to these beautiful, ungainly creatures.

The once and future cow.

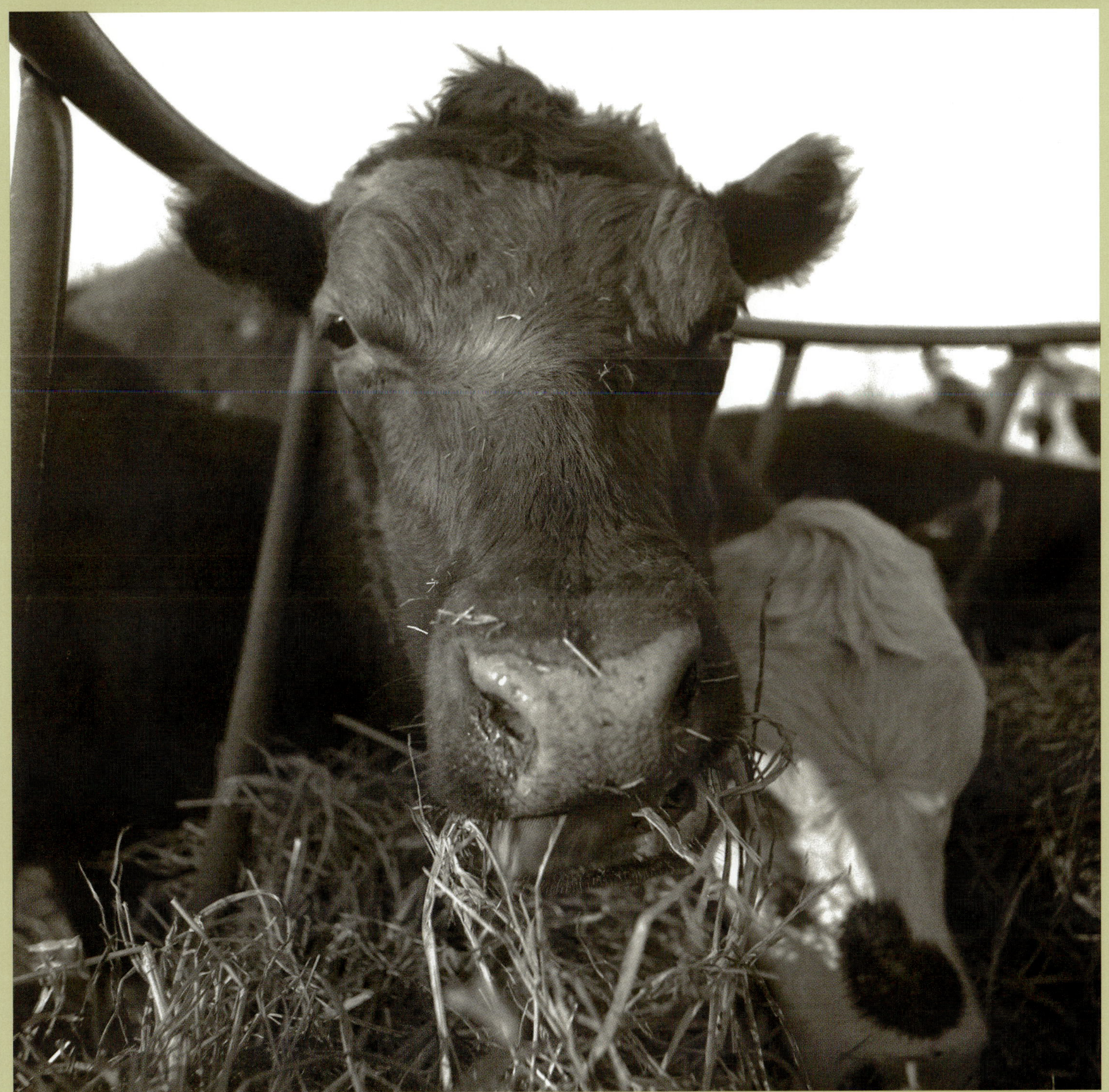

The Misappropriation of Cows

WOMAN REGISTERED COWS AS VOTERS

Brenda Gould is in trouble again for registering her cows as voters.

For the second year running, the woman from Newmarket, near Cambridge in eastern England, has listed two names on the registration form who turned out to be cows.

The previous year, in addition to registering two cows as "Henry and Sophie Bull," she listed "Jake Woofles," later found to be a dog, as eligible to vote in local government elections, the council said.

This year, she indicated that her address had been split into two properties, that she resided in one part and that two other persons lived in the second, a council spokesman said. The persons she claimed lived in the second property were, in fact, her cows.

Gould had been scheduled to appear at Ely Magistrates Court today but did not arrive. She was convicted in her absence and ordered to pay a fine.

— *News.com.au,* From Correspondents in London, February 20, 2004

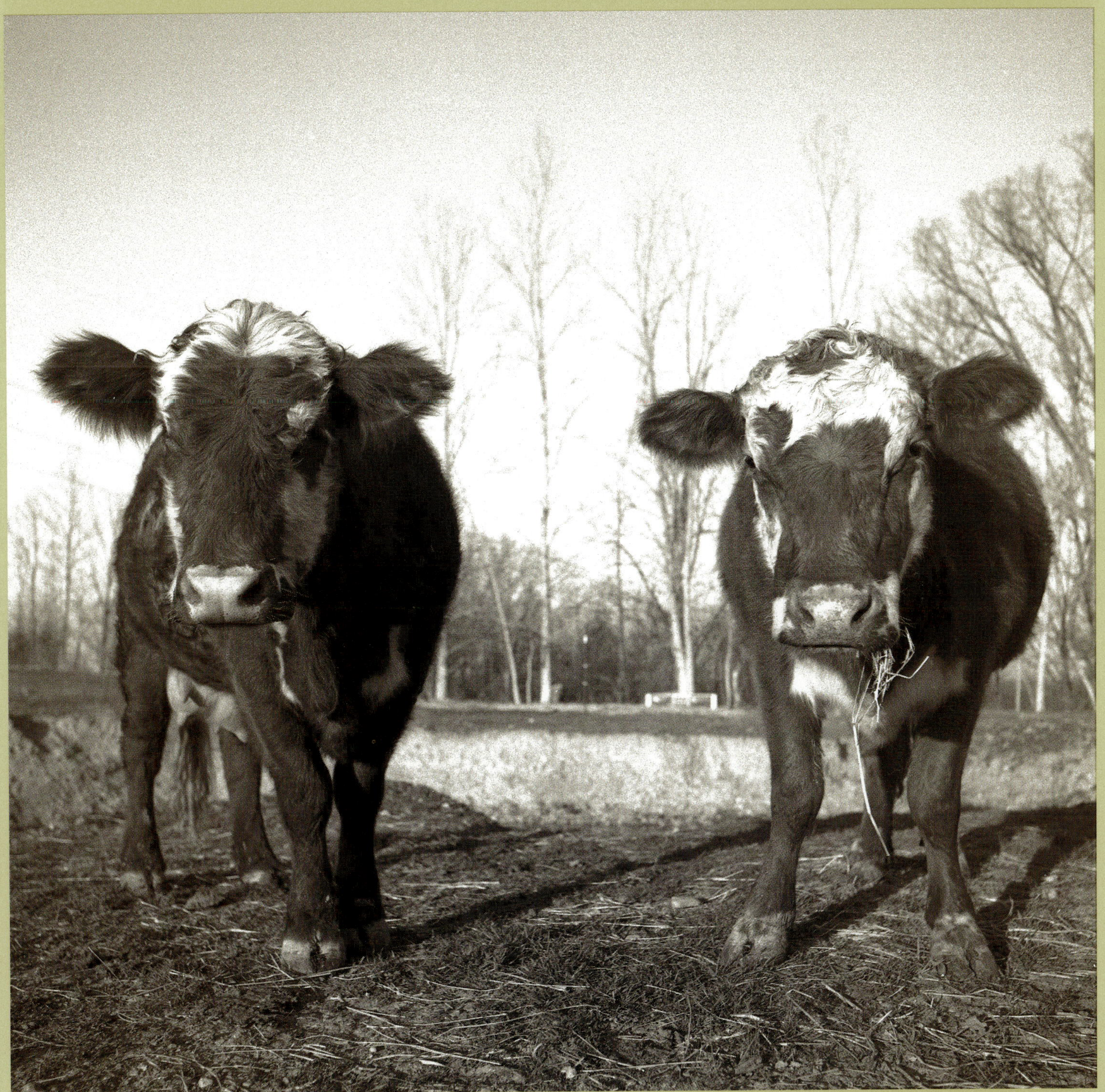

The Disadvantage of Cows

by Ian Tyson

"Cows get a bad deal, Dad." This comment came from my daughter, Adelita, as we drove home from school one day. By "cows" she meant the cross-bred range cow of the Northern Plains. "They're always getting shoved and poked and yelled at."

As she talked, I thought to myself, "That's pretty humane for a little kid." Many ranch kids are dismissive at best concerning livestock, and perhaps they have to be. Some enviros think all the ills of the West can be blamed on cows. That's just numbers and space. On spacious range the thrifty little black cow asks only to be left alone to raise a fine baby every year. She'll walk miles to water and return to mother her calf. Through long northern winters, she toughs out the cold, in the open, on minimal food and water, only to bring another spanking new baby into the frigid world.

Adelita was right.

I like the little black cow.

She's a trouper.

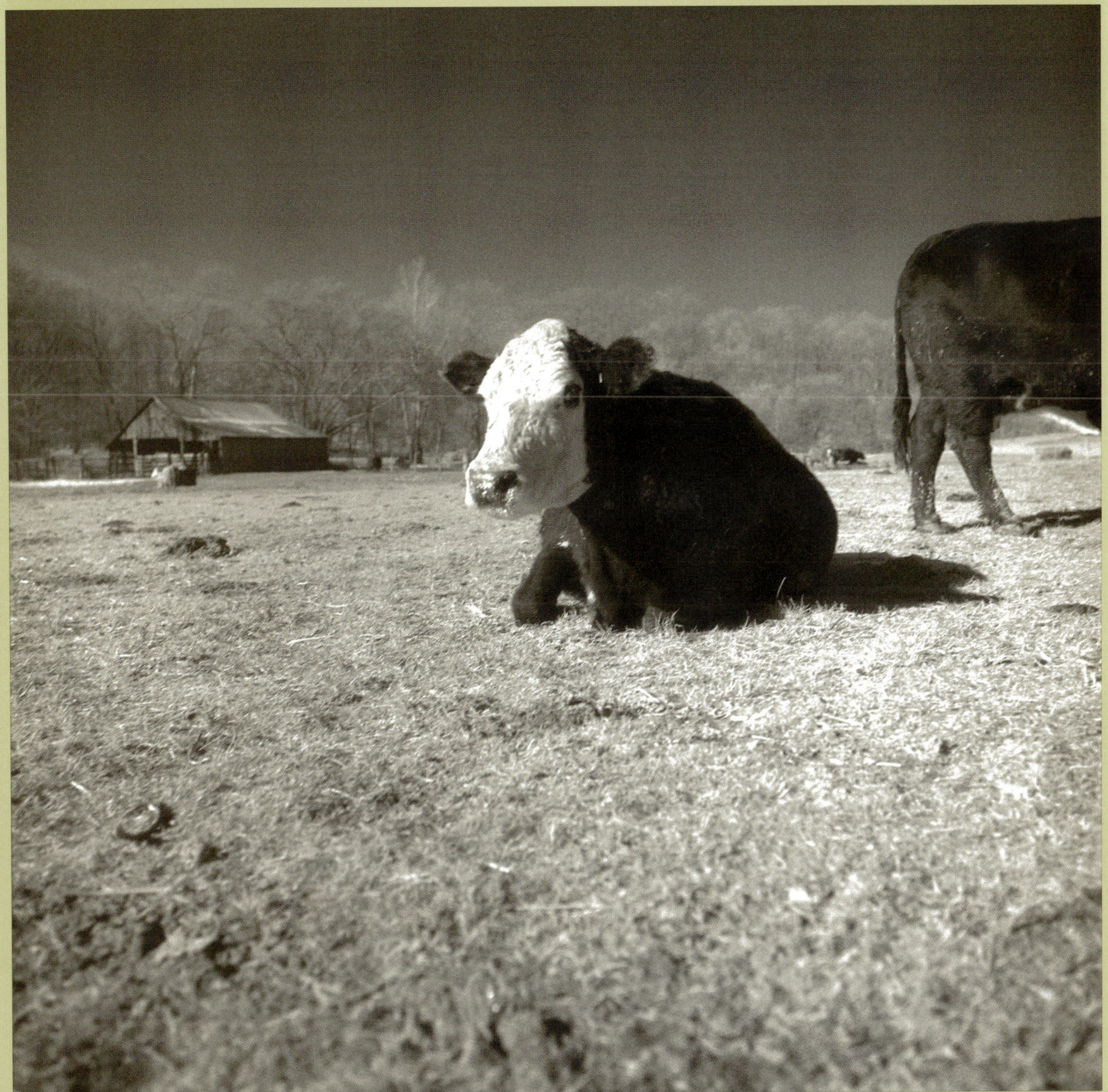

The Family of Cows

The New Cow

The new cow came though the gate,
and her calf came after, a little late.
No longer willing to be led,
the calf went on ahead,
while she stood to look around
over the hills and lower ground
stood shyly, defiantly there,
smelling flower-fragrant air,
and gazed toward the old cows
grouped on the way before.
Knowing not how she might stay
among them, stranger still,
she hesitated yet, now they had turned
at the foot of the hill
and seemed to wait for her at the gate,
to wait for her who was strange and thin,
till she came on,
and they opened their ranks
to take her in.

—August Derleth

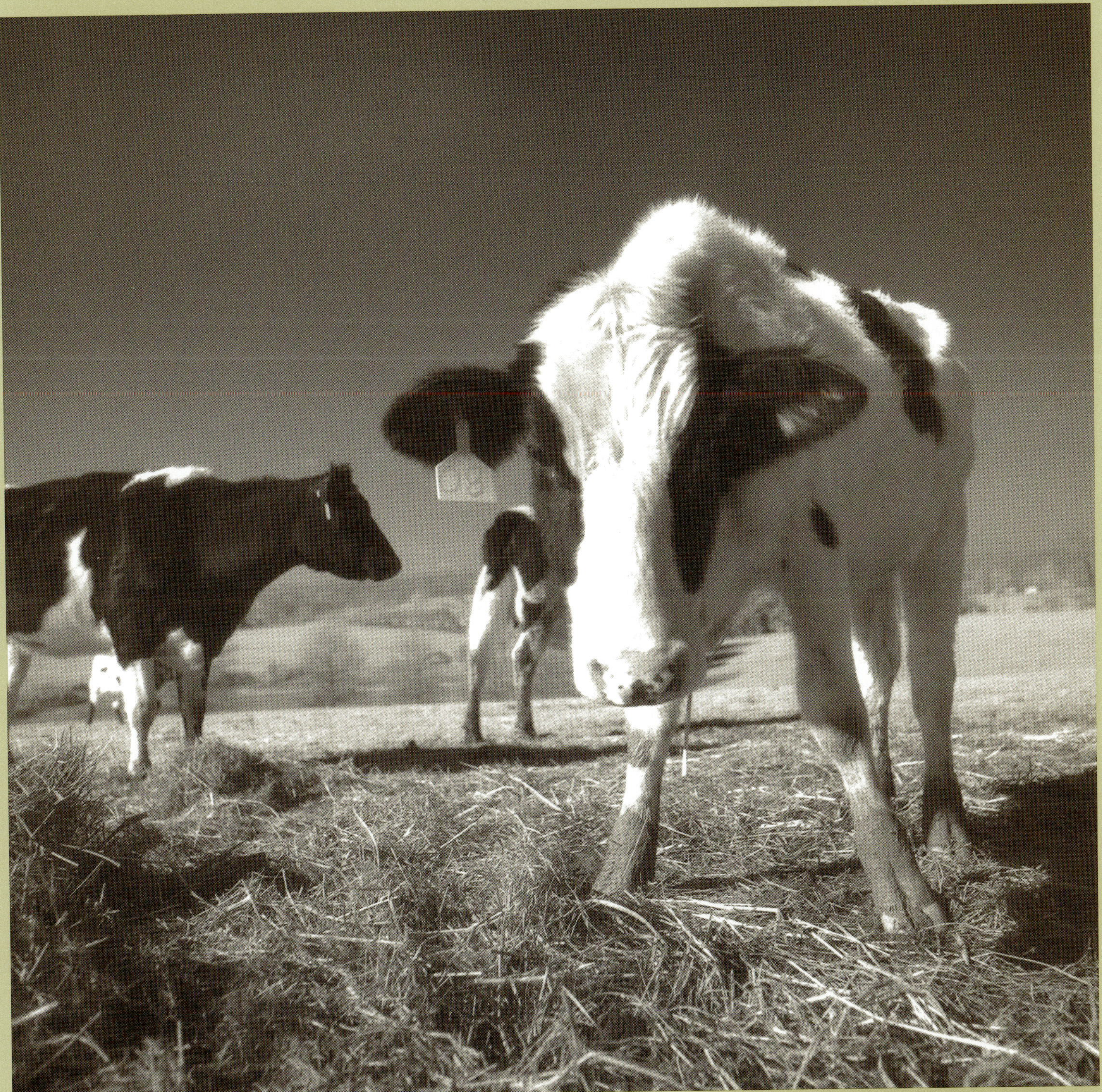
08

The Business of Cows

by Helen Doenz

So you want to milk a cow?

All right, first put her in a stall and secure her head—oh, better feed her some chop so she'll stay put long enough to tie her up. That takes care of that end.

Now to approach the other end! This is the business end. In one hand you have a shiny bucket, and in the other a little one-legged stool, about nine inches high.

Approach the cow from the right-hand side; set the stool down carefully and ease yourself onto it, close enough to the cow so you can lean your head into her flank. Put the bucket down underneath her udder (bag). Now if your hands are cold, you had better push really hard into her flank with your head, or *oops*—one cow's foot goes in the bucket; but maybe not. Grip the two front teats and squeeze, starting with the top fingers and squeeze down—good. You got milk. What a neat sound it makes when it hits the bottom of the pail; a few more squirts and you are getting confident. Smack! One hairy tail lands across your eyes. You react with a slap to the ribs of this unmannerly beast. Oh darn, her one foot is in the bucket.

I guess you should have tied her tail to her off-side leg before you started milking. Go rinse out the pail, tie her tail, and start again. Now you are back on the stool and she knows who's boss! The milk is making a nice foam in the bottom of the bucket. Bossie is chewing her cud. Oh look, there's the kitty. A squirt in his direction might be fun. Bad idea! The rhythm is broken, Bossie jumps away, the stool tips over, the milk spills into the gutter.

All is not lost; there are still the two back teats to milk. Be ready this time. Start again.

Hold the pail between your knees so you can rescue it if necessary.

Get on your stool and put your head in her flank.

Now, forget the cat and keep milking!

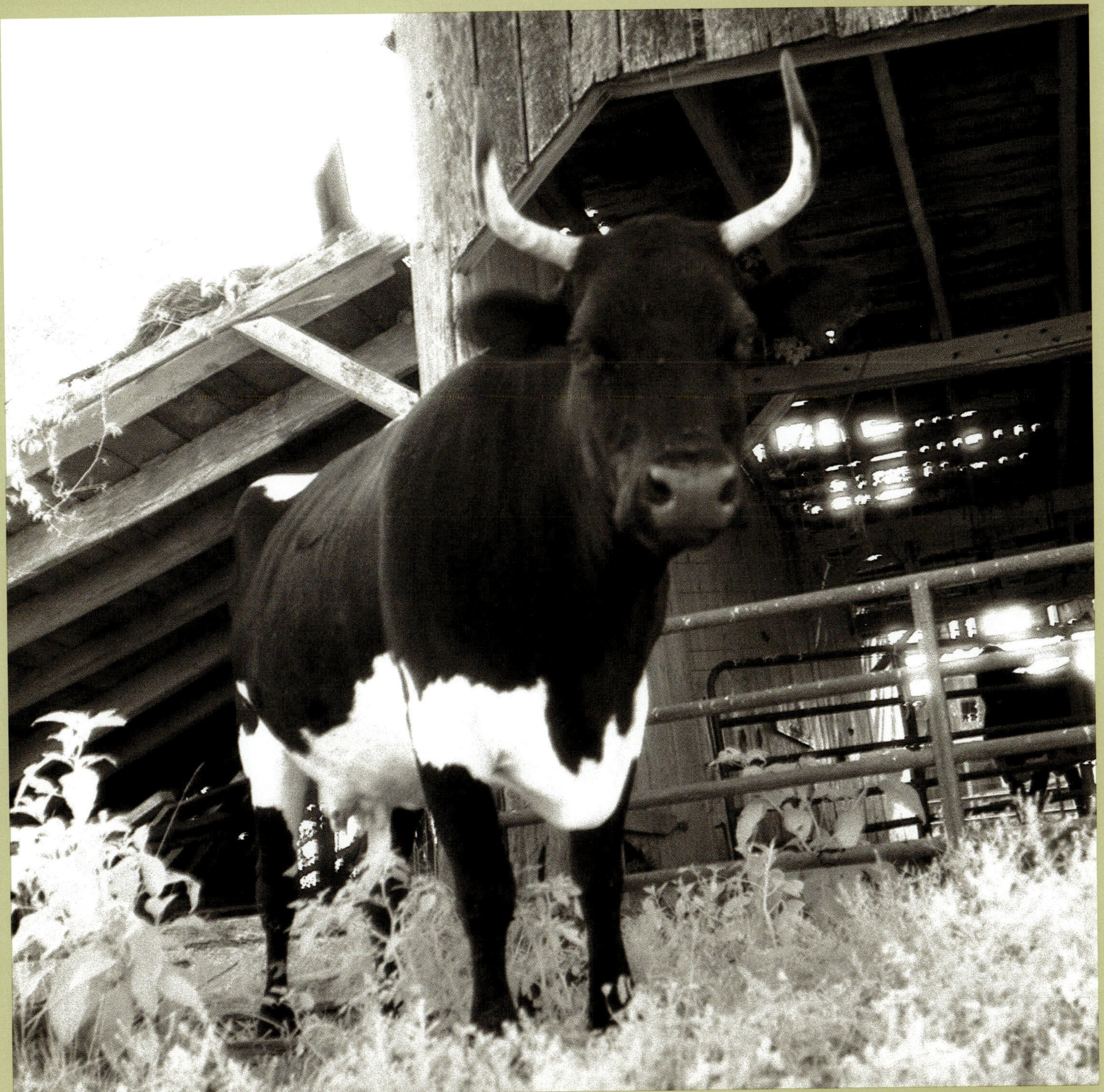

The Sacrifce of Cows

by Jim Glaser

Flossie was the family milk cow.
She always forgave us for stealing her babies,
and robbing her milk for our table.

When I milked her, she would often
turn and stare at me,
large, unblinking brown eyes
full of gentle acceptance.

Then one year her milk dried up,
and we butchered her.

Years later it all came back to me.
I awoke one day, my mind
no longer able to do the mental gymnastics
necessary to separate the meat on my plate
from the process by which it got there.

I'll never eat meat again.
And by the way, Flossie, I'm sorry.

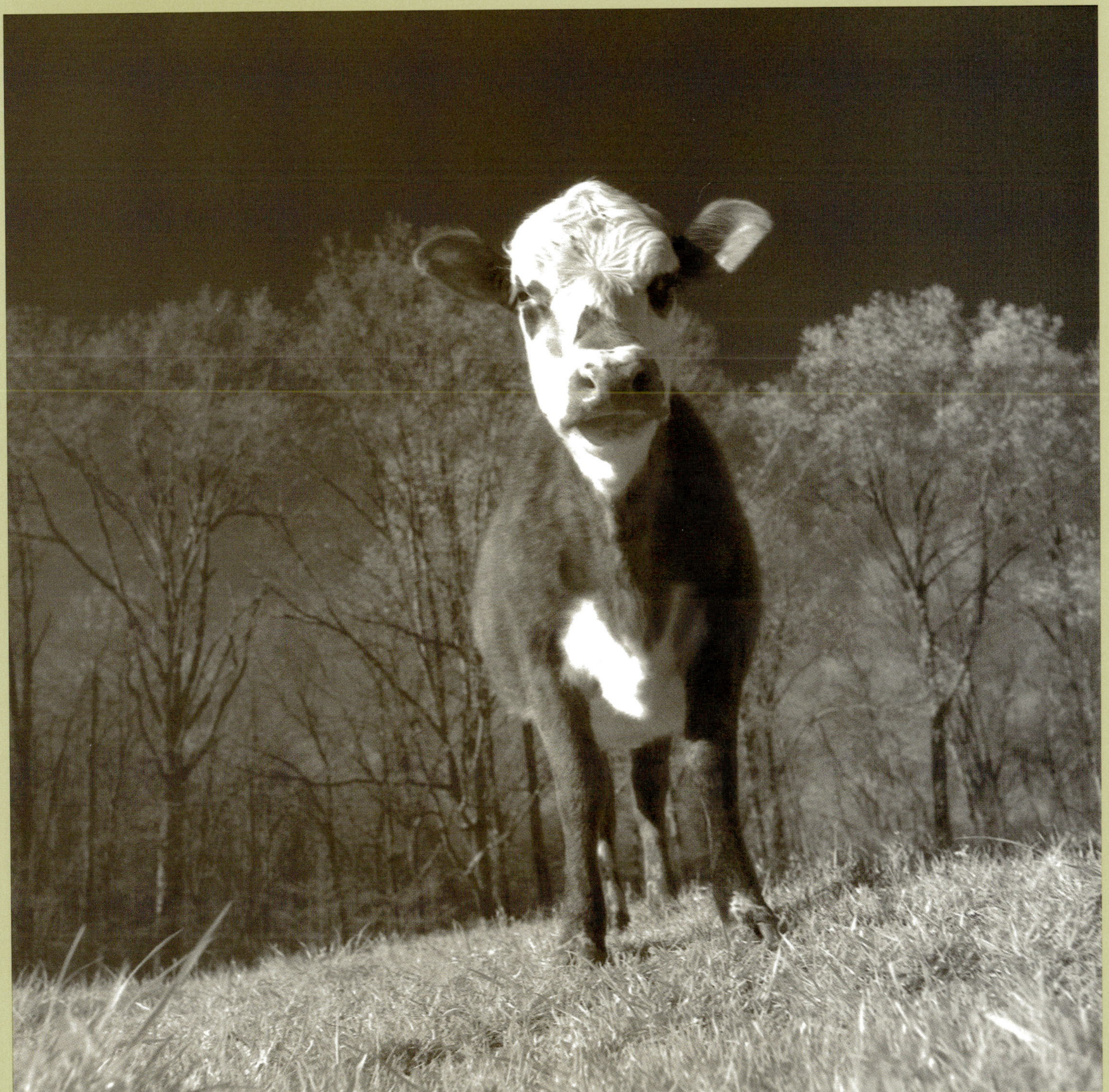

The Trivia of Cows

The word "cow" is among the oldest words known to humankind.

Cows were first domesticated about five thousand years ago.

The first written symbol for "cow" resembled the English letter "A," upside down.

Cows came to America with Christopher Columbus.

A cow averages 41,360 daily jaw movements.

Cows can detect odors up to five miles away.

Of all cow breeds, the Holstein produces the most milk.

The spots on a cow are like human fingerprints, with no two exactly alike.

The cow is a *ruminant,* which means it is an herbivore that chews the cud and has a very complex digestive system with a four-part stomach.

During the day, cows spend 6 hours eating and 8 hours chewing their cuds. It drinks about 30 gallons of water per day

There are approximately 350 squirts in a gallon of milk.

There are 52 different cow breeds in America, and 920 in the world.

An average cow can live up to 25 years. Its age can be determined by counting the rings on its horns.

A cow stands up and sits down on an average of 14 times a day.

The design of Boston was laid out according to cow paths.

On the island of Sardinia, in the town of Sassari, is one of the island's most famous Romanesque shrines. As local legend tells it, a cow used to kneel at a certain spot every day, as if deep in prayer. Thus a church was built where the cow knelt. Its name is Church of the Trinity of the Spotted Cow.

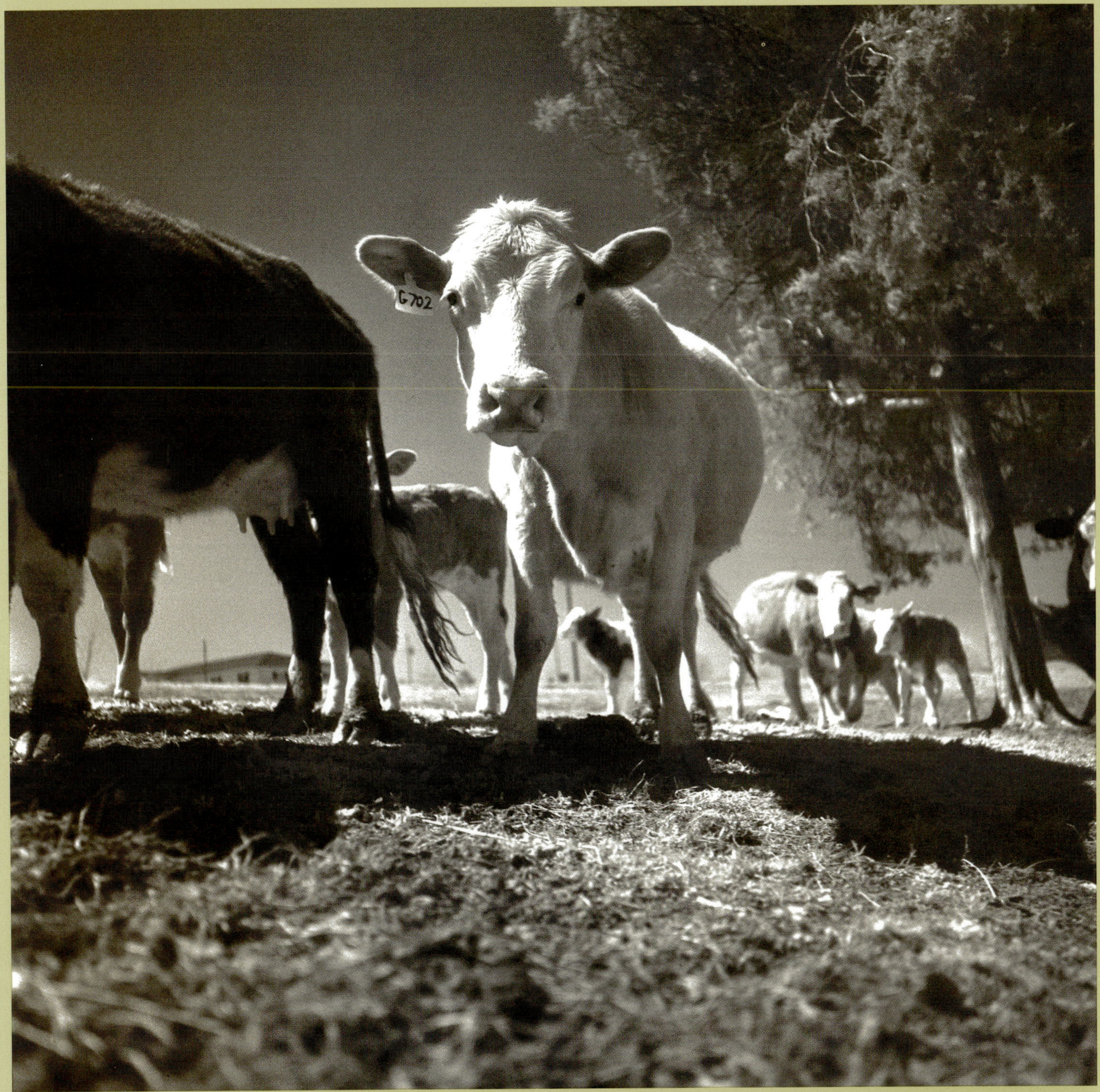
G702

The Politics of Cows

"If he wants to come and see some cows,
he's welcome to come out there and see some cows."

President George W. Bush, to *Paris Match* magazine,
about whether or not he'd invite French President Chirac to Texas.

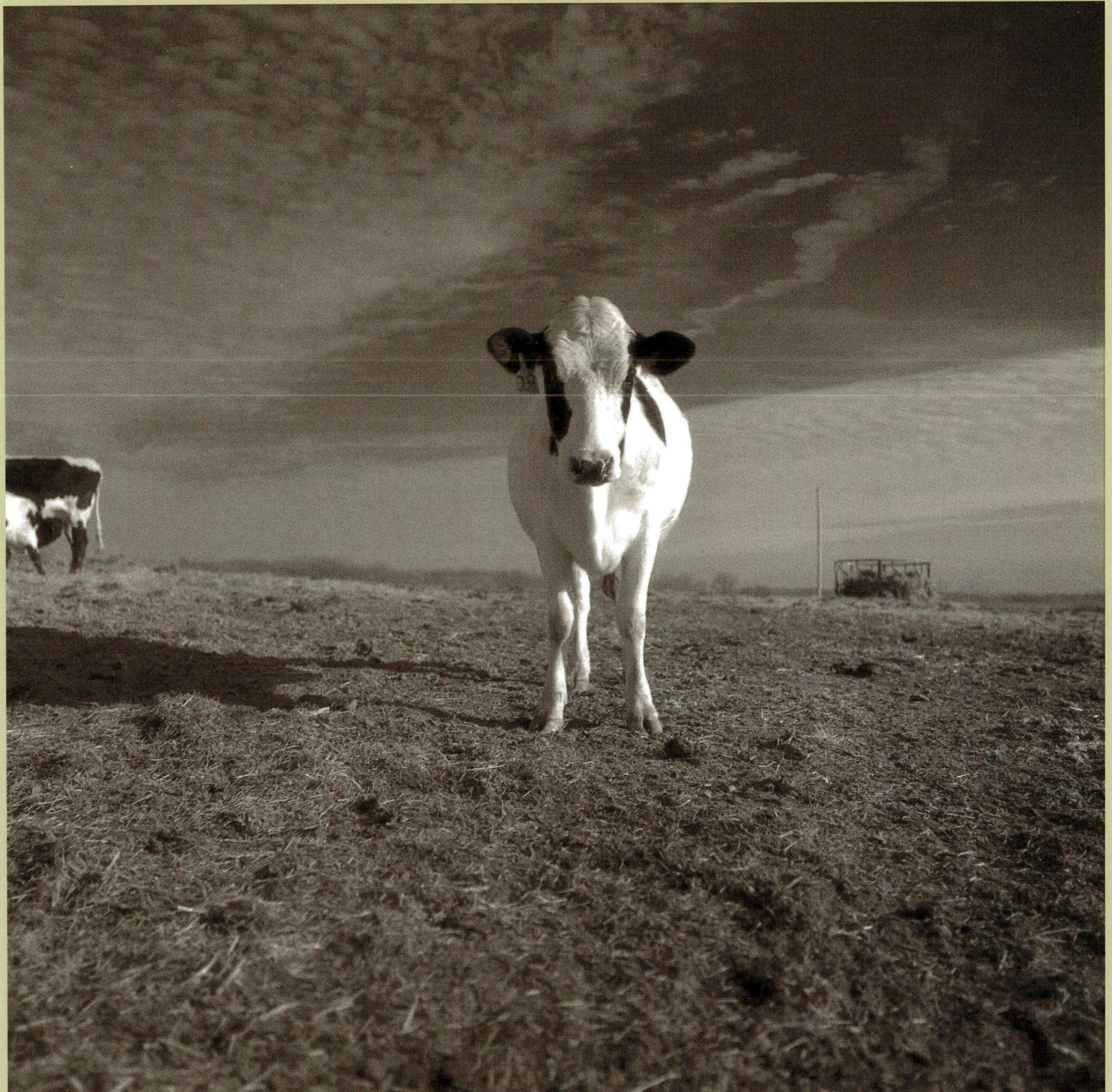

The Breath of Cows

by Sandy Richardson

Outside, thunder grumbles, lightning flashes. The rain spits and spats on the windowsill, running in streams over the ledge and down the side of my study wall. The sounds and smells of these summer storms always take me back to childhood, the musty smell of my grandmother's old house and the earthy scent of the yard, and of freshly mowed grass and spring onions.

My grandmother, Nannie, would call me inside from the storm, and we'd curl up together on the bed by the open window. Most often during those storms, Nannie read to me, and then we'd lie quietly, listening, breathing in time with each other while the thunder rumbled and the lightning flashed. "The angels are moving God's furniture around, and the devil's cracking his whip," she'd explain. But the green smells and her gentle voice calmed and soothed me, in spite of the noise.

Today's storm also reminds me of Martha, our milk cow. Always nervous during a storm, she often interrupted Nannie and me by galumphing as fast as she could to the bedroom window, and stretching the rope that tethered her in the side yard. There was just enough rope to allow her to reach the window and rub her wet nose against the screen, pushing against it so hard there was a permanent sag in the center. Her brown eyes would roll with each rumble and crack from above, while her body rocked from side to side against the house siding where she had already worn away the paint.

But even when the noises settled and the rain slowed, Martha remained at the window, blowing gentle puffs of air through the screen, watching us with wide eyes, her ears alert for the soft murmuring of Nannie's voice. "She's a right smart cow," Nannie always commented, and I would nod, believing that Martha, like me, got lost in the wonder of those stories my grandmother taught me to love.

When the storm was spent and the story done, Nannie rose to finish the hundred chores that filled her days, and Martha plodded back to her place under the tree, content to nibble at what grew beneath. As for me, I slept dreamlessly, perfectly at peace, cradled on one side by the lingering warmth of my grandmother's body and, on the other, by the memory of Martha's sweet breath.

I have lost both Nannie and Martha now. But regardless of the years between then and now, today's summer storm and an open window brought them back. Nannie is beside me; Martha at the screen. And I am home again. Safe. Secure. Cradled in love.

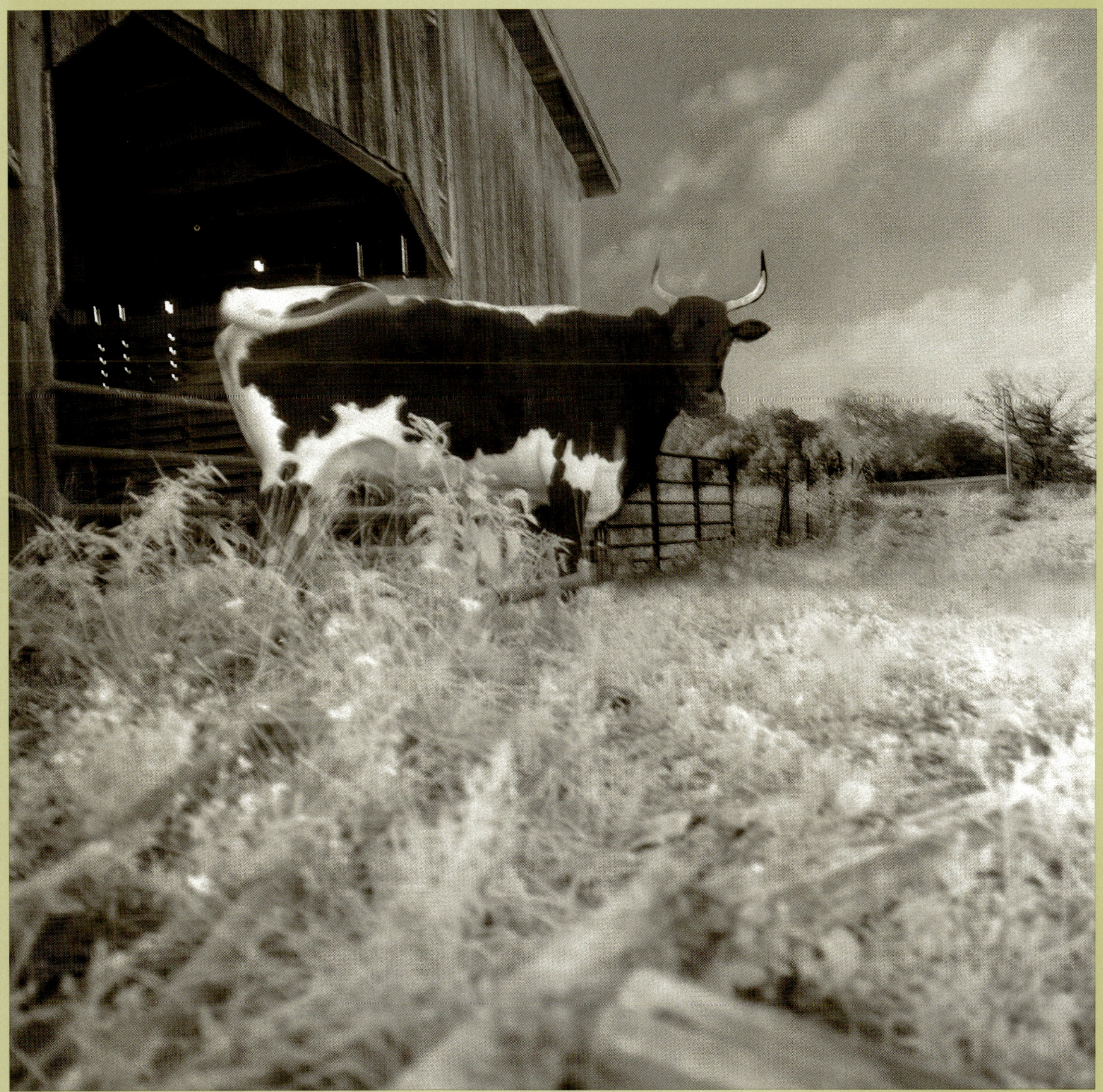

The Forgetfulness of Cows

by George Rodrigue

As a young kid, during the summers of 1956 through 1959, I worked at my uncle's dairy farm, Boutte's Fresh Milk, in the country near New Iberia, Louisiana. It was my job to herd the cows from the pastures into the dairy, where the men would hook them up to the brand new milking machines.

Usually, my cousin Arlene joined me. She was a real horse girl and insisted we make a contest out of herding the cows. One day as we raced, my horse went over a ditch where it had always turned right in the past. As the horse landed on the other side, I flew into the mud, where cows waiting for direction soon surrounded me, as though they honestly didn't remember the way to the barn.

One thing about a cow: when it's time to get milked, it can't think of anything else.

While the machines milked the cows, Arlene and I enjoyed my uncle's swimming pool, the only pool in New Iberia. We called it "the cement pond," because the water was black. When the cows were finished, we'd jump on the horses, still wearing our bathing suits, and escort the cows through the gates and roads to the back pasture—not an easy job with forty or fifty head of cattle. We always managed somehow.

The other exciting thing I remember about the farm was that my uncle had the first air-conditioned car in New Iberia, a gray Hudson. But the cows never got to ride in it.

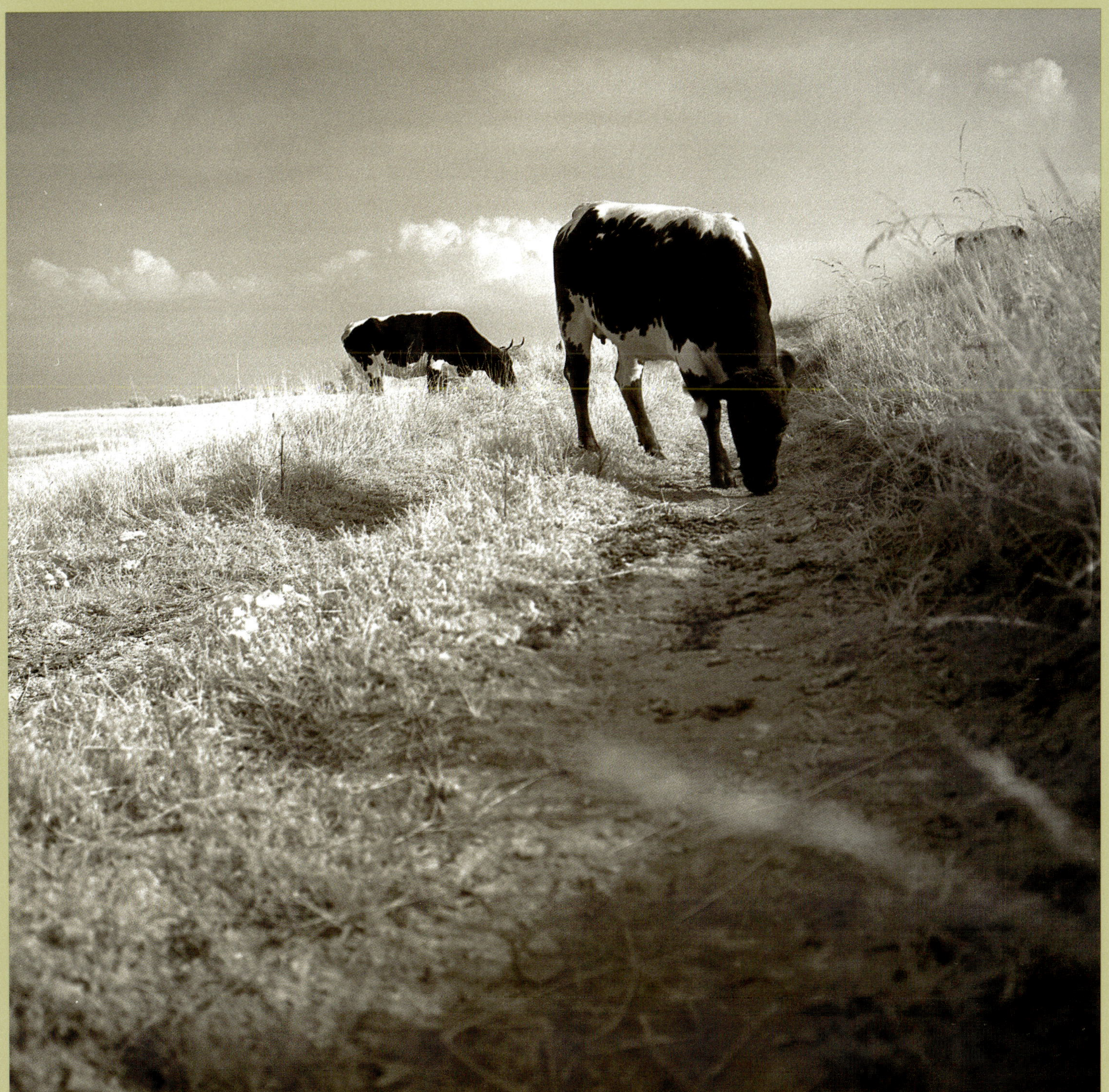

The Ancestry of Cows

"They are but a little less than elephants in size, and are of the species, color, and form of a bull. Their strength is very great, and also their speed. They spare neither man nor beast that they see. They cannot be brought to endure the sight of men, nor be tamed, even when taken young. The people, who take them in pitfalls, assiduously destroy them; and young men harden themselves in this labor, and exercise themselves in this kind of chase; and those who have killed a great number—the horns being publicly exhibited in evidence of the fact—obtain great honor. The horns, in amplitude, shape, and species, differ much from the horns of our oxen. They are much sought after; and after having been edged with silver at their mouths they are used for drinking vessels at great feasts."

Julius Caesar, in his diary, on seeing aurochs, the ancestor of cows, for the first time in the German Black Forest.

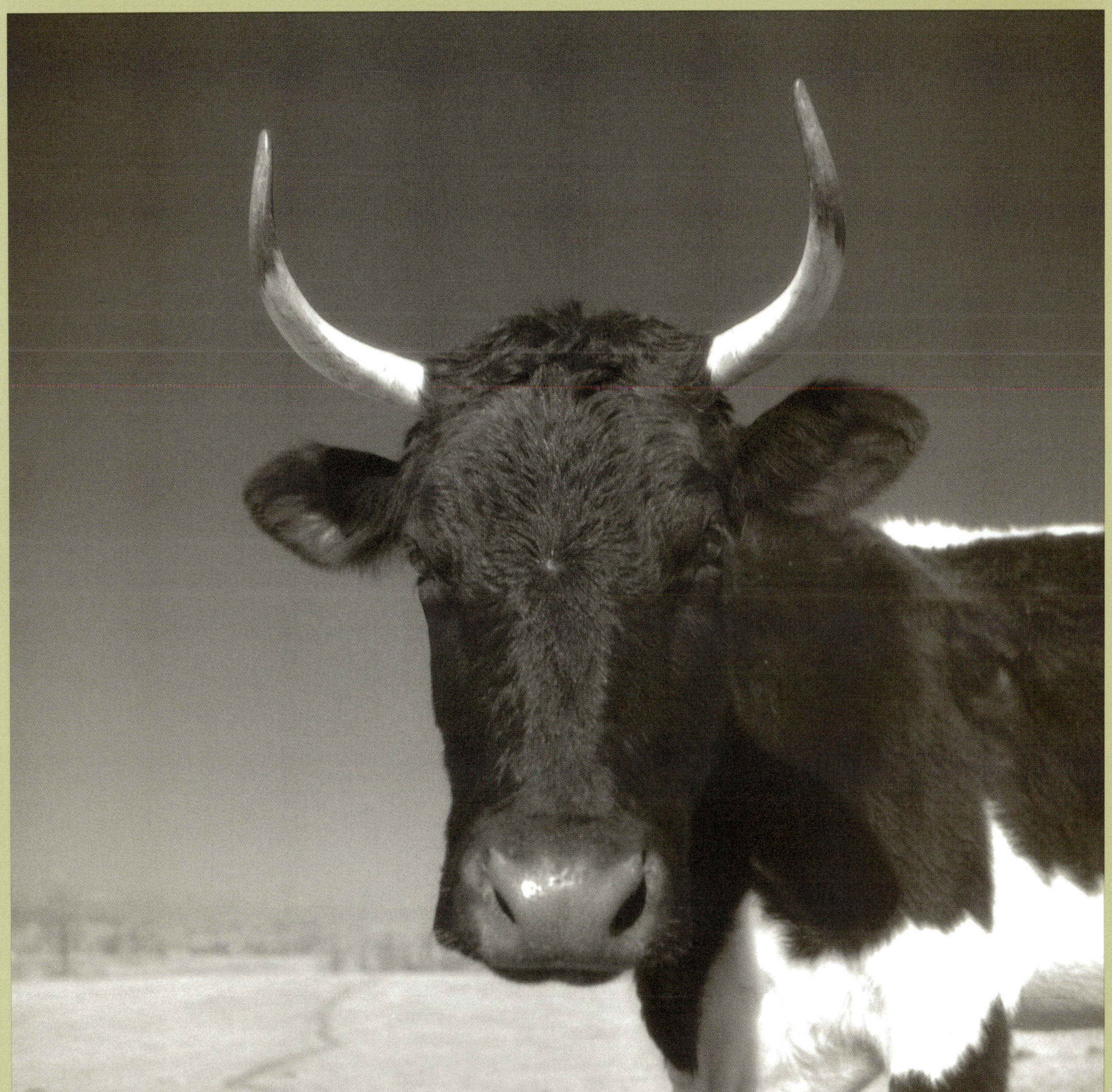

The Loyalty of Cows

by Sandra Adelmund

This poem is a reminiscence of my first honeymoon, in Vermont. I came across a cow in a pasture, and I started talking to it. She turned toward me and I threw her a kiss. That cow reminded me of the cows I had known as a child growing up on an acreage at the edge of town, back in Iowa. I'm a vegetarian now. I'd rather throw a cow a kiss.

Watching the Milk Cows

It's probably vain
we watch them
thinking how much
we're needed, how little
our houses mean when compared
to warm straw and lantern light.
We remember our rural beginnings:
how streets were graveled—not paved
how the errant cow—routed by flood waters—
carries with it into daybreak some secret country
we once called home. How long into the
night we'll dream them, soft and full
of milk, cooing to us, chewing their cuds,
so much trust in their eyes
it makes us squirm.

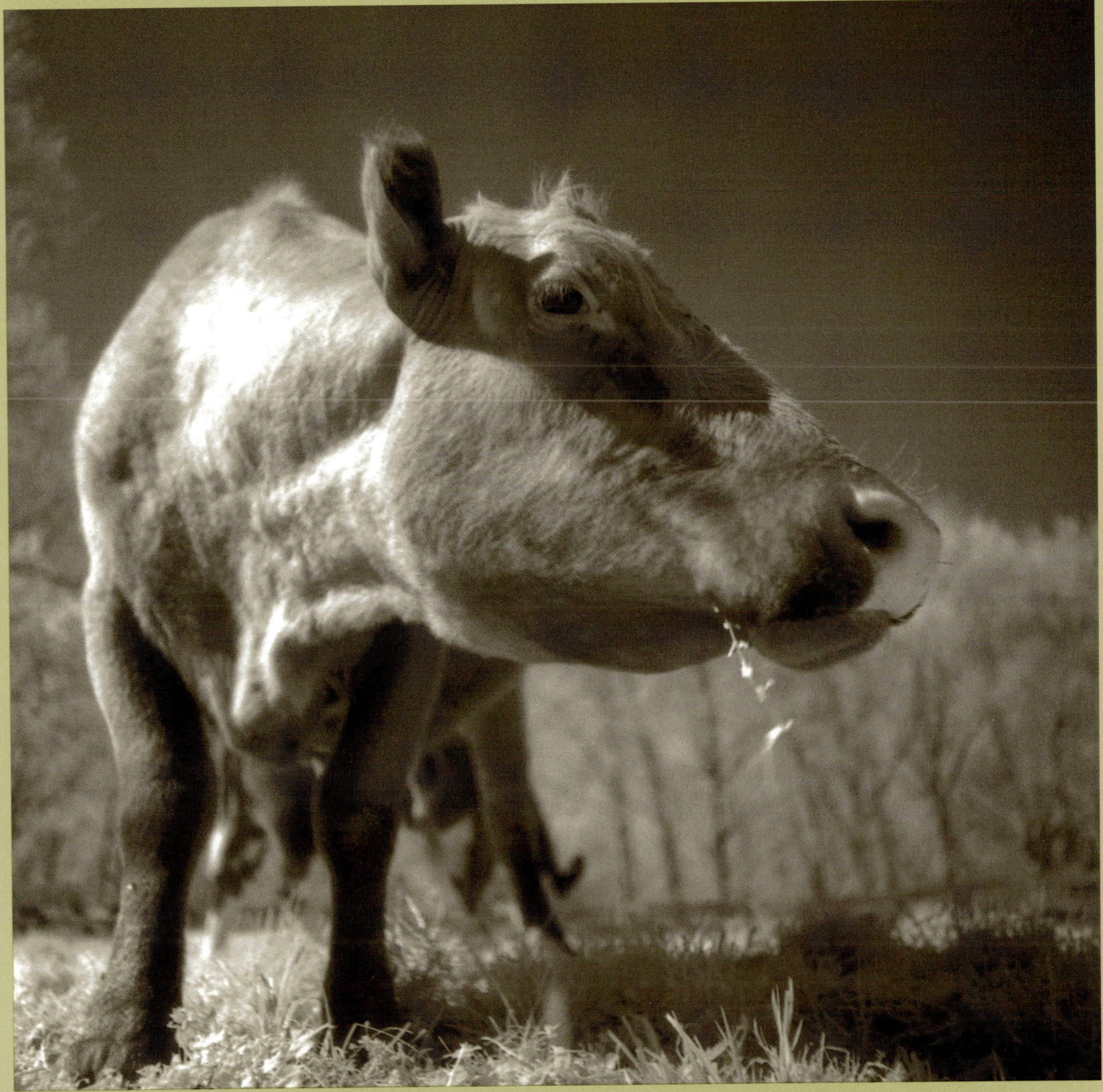

The Challenge of Cows

by Michael McNeilly

At ten years old, I had an imagination that caused me grief when I was alone at night. This was the same active imagination that went with me deep into the woods where I lived. I was certain the trees harbored monsters that could and would slide down my back and eat me alive.

One memory stands out, in those same woods, at a spot where one dirt path was divided by barbed fences on either side. Each of those fields was commanded by a huge bull. One on each side. They were enormous. Their size was not a product of my imagination, but of the rich alfalfa that the Mississippi flood lands grew in that area in Southern Illinois.

There was a devil wind howling that night, and I had been clinging to a walnut tree for protection, praying that nothing would dine on my flesh. When it was time to make a run for home, I let go of the tree and fled, screaming, as fast as ten-year-old, size-eleven feet could carry me. (My nickname back then was Feet.)

When my big feet hit the road, I was stopped by a sound too deep to be human. There, on each side of the path, staring at each other, were the two black monsters themselves. Their grunts and breaths mingled together to form a visible sound not unlike the language of the Horned One himself. I stood, frozen, just on the edge of their line of combat, and their hatred of each other. With each grunt they would push the barbed wire into their shoulders, moving it forward by inches. This was a power I had never witnessed before. This was a life-threatening dilemma: Behind me, the crazed Wind Murderer ... before me, the Minions of the Fence. They were the razor-wired gauntlet I had to pass through in order to live. No going back. And maybe Death to go forward.

This moment in my childhood is etched forever in my memory. When I look back on it, I realize that the "going forward" meant so much to me. I was a boy caught between two mad bulls, but a boy going on. A boy facing up to scary things. I did it. I owe a lot to cows.

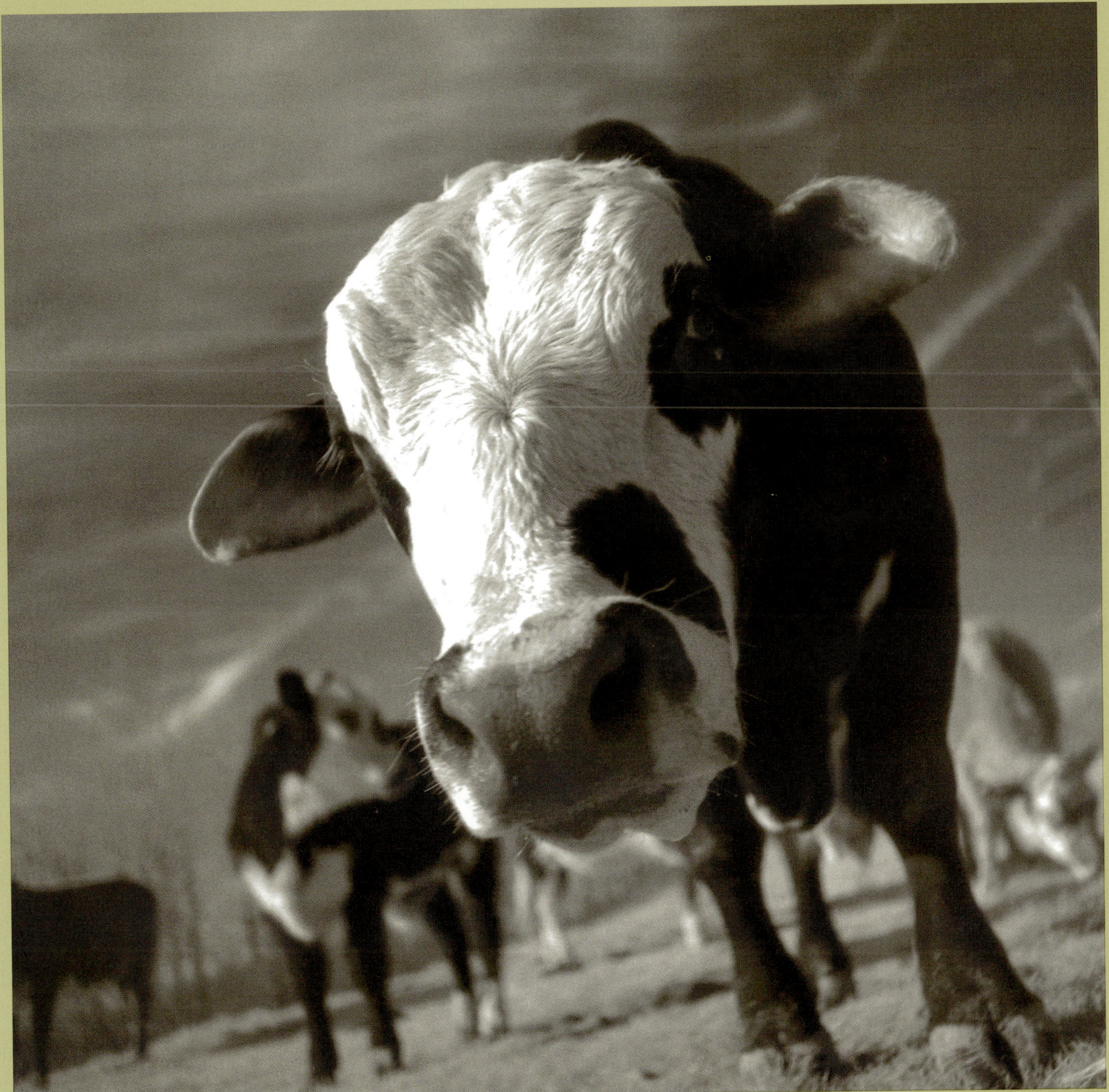

The Immortality of Cows

by Charles Fishman

I had a poetry residency at the Virginia Center for the Creative Arts in June 1997. At the time, a herd of cows grazed on a grassy hillside near a narrow road that wound its way upward toward the sleeping quarters and studios of the resident artists. One evening after dark, I drove back to VCCA from Sweetbriar College, which was a short distance away. At night, the cows exerted a presence that was charged with otherness and tinged with danger. I was drawn by the force the herd of cows exerted but also wary of their power, and the subtle menace that seemed to hover around them like a nimbus. This poem grew out of that experience.

Cows at Night

They are the black
and white souls
of the dead—
did you think
that souls
were colorless,
the transparent
and diaphanous cloth
that drapes
the movie phantoms?
When they hug
the long drive
that leads
to your habitation,
know they have
something
other than mortal
to tell you: theirs
will be a notion
that cannot be put
into words.
That huddling
and posturing
they do—the flared
eye, the head
held steady as stone—
it is for you.
That haunted hovering
over the black skin
of the earth—
for you.

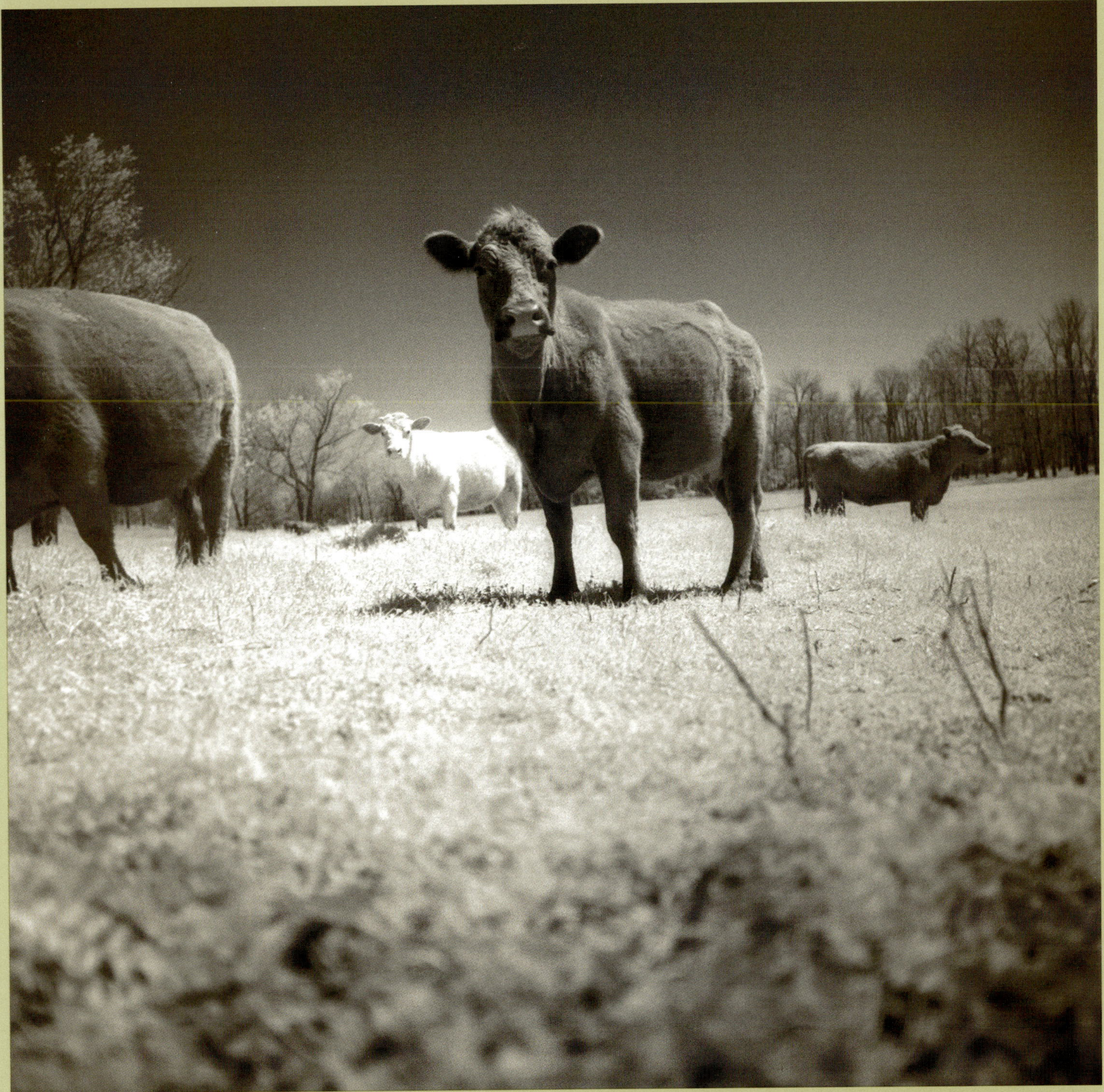

The Memory of Cows

by Cathie Pelletier

They forget nothing. You can see it in their eyes, which hold the wisdom of tribal elders. They have been busy all those years standing in open fields, or lying in the thin shade of the cottonwoods, or leaning against the barn stall in the dim light of February. We might think they are merely waiting, as always, for the inevitable, but we would be wrong. This is the time cows spend remembering, all through those summer rainstorms, the winter snowstorms, those years of buttercups and daisies, fallen acorns and red leaves.

They remember the farmer who gave them hay, the cut of his green hat against the evening sky, the sharp smell of tobacco as he would shout, "Get in there now, go on!" pushing them toward the two open arms of the welcoming barn. This is the farmer who, one day as the cows watched, went down on his knees by the salt lick, hands to his chest, heart exploding beneath the sweat of his shirt. The one who then lay on his back, eyes open as if seeing clouds for the first time, the cows gathering around, gently nuzzling his face, knowing that the last thing he would ever feel on earth would be their whiskers, light as raindrops on his skin.

They remember the children, gone now to jobs in the tall buildings of some city, their tire swing rotting in the lower pasture.

They remember the woman who came each week to dump the bucket, apple peels curling like sweet, red smiles along the ground.

They remember the city people who stopped their cars and stared, leaning on the fence, ready to run at the first quick swish of tail, a sudden kick of hoof against earth.

They remember the lovers who arrived one night to lie on the grass beneath the same cottonwoods, a great horned owl perched against the moon, the smell of perfume and gin.

They remember the string of cars that sped past each day, rain or shine, humans hurrying toward some great and useless notion.

Keepers of the flame, cows give us the courage to say good-bye, for they remember the truth about our lives. Yet, they share this knowledge with no one, not even each other.

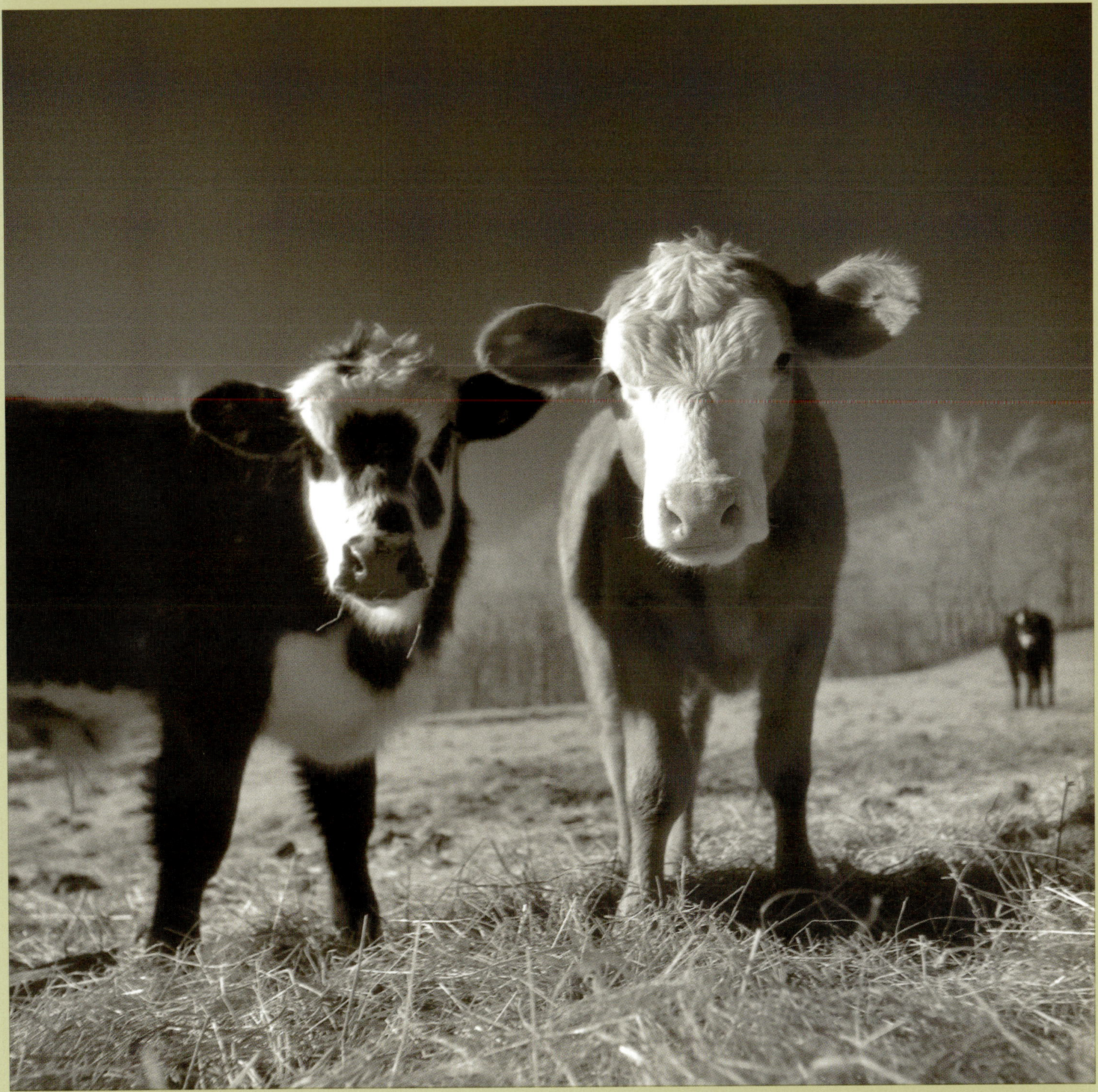

The Scent of Cows

by Rick Hautala

I love the smell of cow manure in the morning. They say that the sense of smell is the strongest trigger of memory, more than sight, touch, sound, or taste. (But I'd wager taste is a close second because it's so close to smell.) When I was growing up, the neighbor's cow barn wasn't more than a hundred yards from my house ... and my bedroom window. I heard the cattle lowing and stomping in their stalls all the time. Often, my friends and I would run through the cow field, imagining that we were matadors and taunting the cows to chase us. (I wonder if we spoiled their milk.)

If I ever want to go back in time to my childhood, all I need is the smell of cow manure, especially on a hot summer morning.

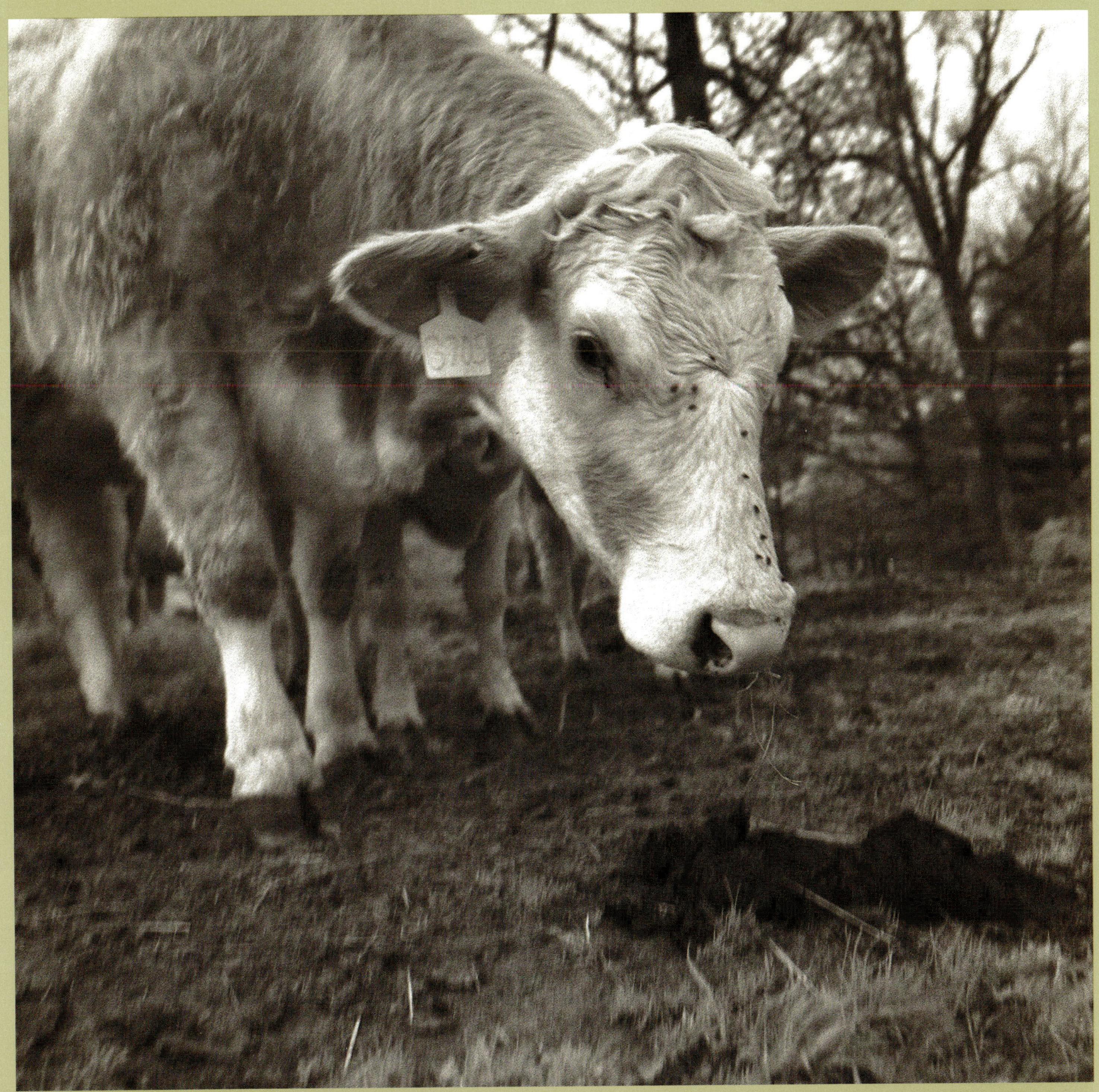

The History of Cows

I am one of the old-timers that went up the old Chisholm Trail. I was born June 18, 1864, in Burnet County, Texas. I started from Burnet in May, 1882, with 3,000 head of steers, owned by Hudson & Watson. Our trail boss was John Christian, also of Burnet. We went north and crossed the Red River at Doan's Store. There we laid over two weeks for two more trail herds to overtake us which belonged to the same men, Hudson & Watson.

When the two herds arrived we threw all three herds together, which made about 9,000 head of cattle. There were to be 4,000 head of *icked cattle to be cut out of this herd. We started cutting out this number in the afternoon. By evening we had 500 head cut out, and my boss and his men took these cattle to hold that night. The other two bosses and their men took the remaining 8,500 cattle to stand guard around.

At sundown when we bedded the cattle down for the night, there were eleven trail herds in sight. Along in the night a terrible storm came up. It was the worst that I ever experienced. The thunder, lightning, and rain was awful. All the cattle were turned loose except small cuts we were holding.

The following morning cattle were dotting the plains in every direction as far as the eye could see. All the trail herds were mixed up. After we had finished our breakfast we started to make the big roundup. There were about 120 cowboys. When we had the roundup made, we had about 33,000 head in one bunch. We worked about ten days before we got the cattle shaped up to start on our way. One of the herds went to Caldwell, Kansas, and one to Cheyenne, Wyoming. The herd I was with went north of Cheyenne.

From Doan's Store we went on through the Indian Nation to Dodge City, Kansas, then on to Ogallala, Nebraska, where we crossed to the South Platte River. We passed through Fort Fetimon and Fort Laramie and went northwest into Wyoming. We were on the trail four-and-one-half months, and had to stand guard every night.

I now own a cow ranch near Williams, Arizona, and I have been here twenty-eight years.

From *Trail Drivers of Texas*, by W.M. Nagiller.

**panicked*

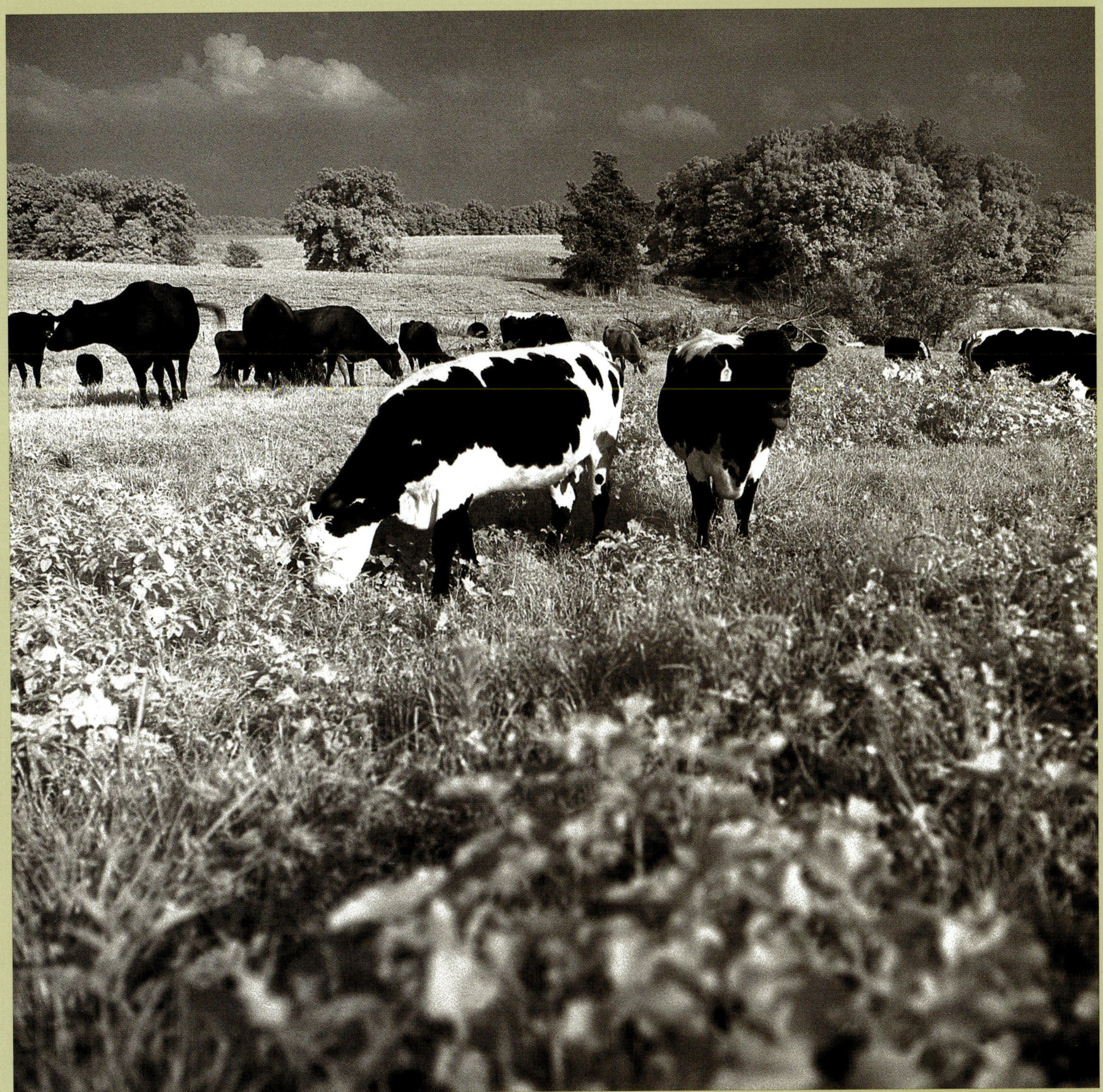

The Divinity of Cows

The Lord is the protector of cows and the Brahminical culture. A society devoid of cow protection and Brahminical culture is not under the direct protection of the Lord, just as the prisoners in the jails are not under the protection of the king but under the protection of a severe agent of the king. Without cow protection and cultivation of the Brahminical qualities in human society, at least for a section of the members of society, no human civilization can prosper at any length.

We must tend the cows very nicely so that they give us sufficient milk.

And with that milk we shall live.

From the writings of His Divine Grace A.C. Bhaktivedanta Swami Prabhupada

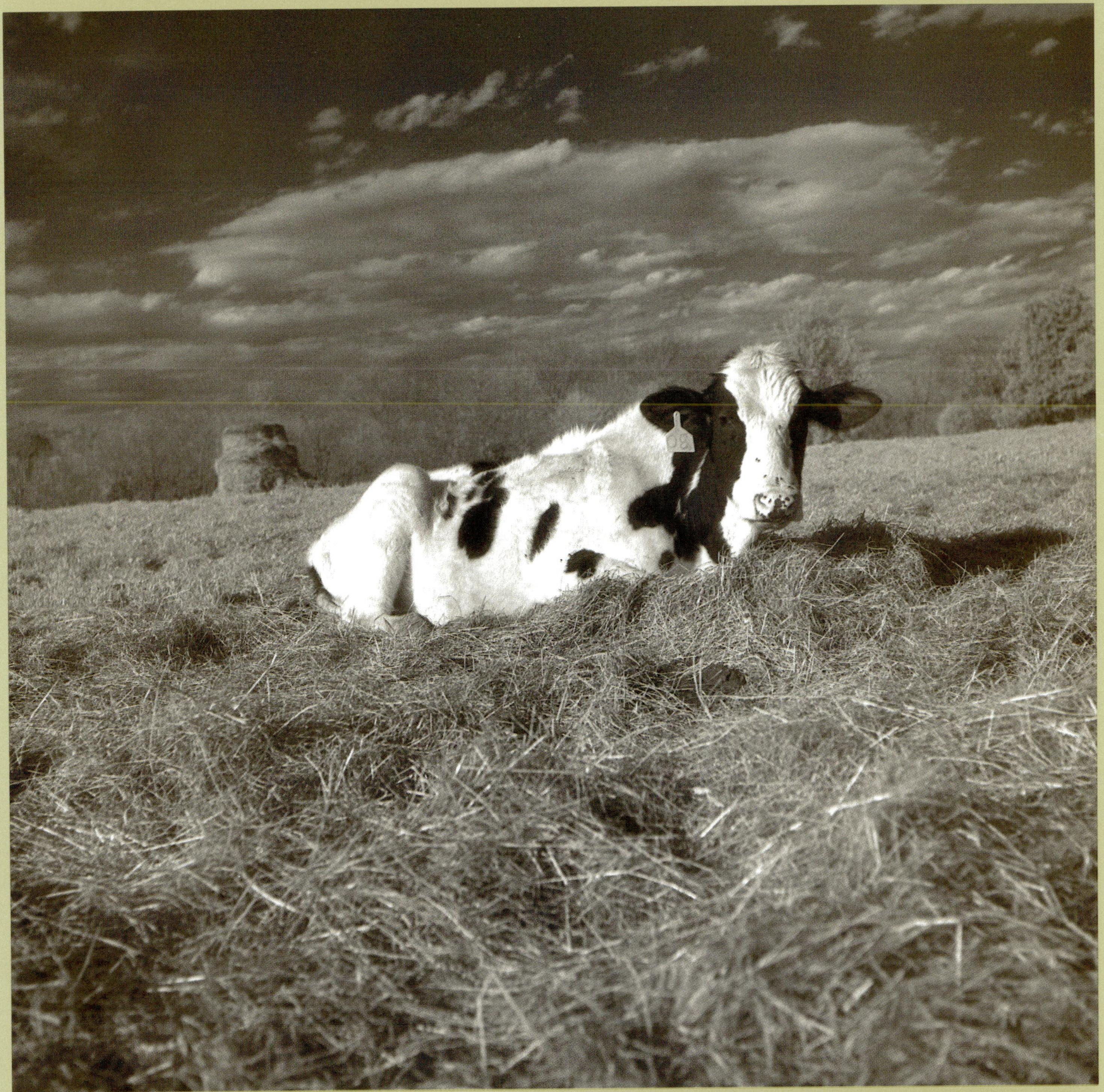

The Rustling of Cows

by Patsi Bale Cox

Friends have informed me that the following "cow story" is now part of popular culture, a joke in areas of the country where certain ethnic groups preside. But I'm here to tell you it started in Hays, Kansas, back in 1966 or 1967. Here's why.

In the Great Plains states such as Kansas, Colorado, Nebraska, and the Dakotas, there resides a wonderful family of immigrants known as "Volga Germans." They are Germans who first settled in Russia under the reign of German-born Catherine the Great, only to leave when they were asked to fight a series of what they considered ill-conceived Russian wars. Because they raised wheat and cattle, America's heartland offered their best hope.

My first contact with this colorful crowd came when I started college at Fort Hays State in 1963. Many of my friends were local girls, and every one of them swore their grandparents still held to "the old ways." The younger Volga Germans had great stories about their families that almost always ended in a punch line delivered in a delightful style of speaking that my friends dubbed: "Volga Chur-man."

One thing I learned on meeting this older generation was that they remained fiercely proud of their heritage. They are industrious and hard working. But the characteristic that I most admired about the Volga Germans was that they did not suffer fools gladly. And because of that I came away from college with a story of my own.

I was a junior, living in an apartment with one of my sorority sisters. One evening I returned home from class just in time to catch the six o'clock news. The lead story was about the latest in a rash of cattle rustlings in the county, and one only needed hear the name of the farmer to know he was a Volga "Chur-man." A young, over-eager television reporter went on a bit relaying the sad tale of these latest missing cows, reminding viewers of similar events in the past few months and asking for help from an alert citizenry. The elderly farmer who stood beside the young man waited patiently for a question. Finally, with great drama, the reporter thrust the microphone in the old man's face.

"And just when did you know your cattle had been rustled?" the young man inquired breathlessly.

The old man arched an eyebrow and studied the reporter closely, incredulously. Finally he said: "Ven I looked for the cows, and there they was ... gone."

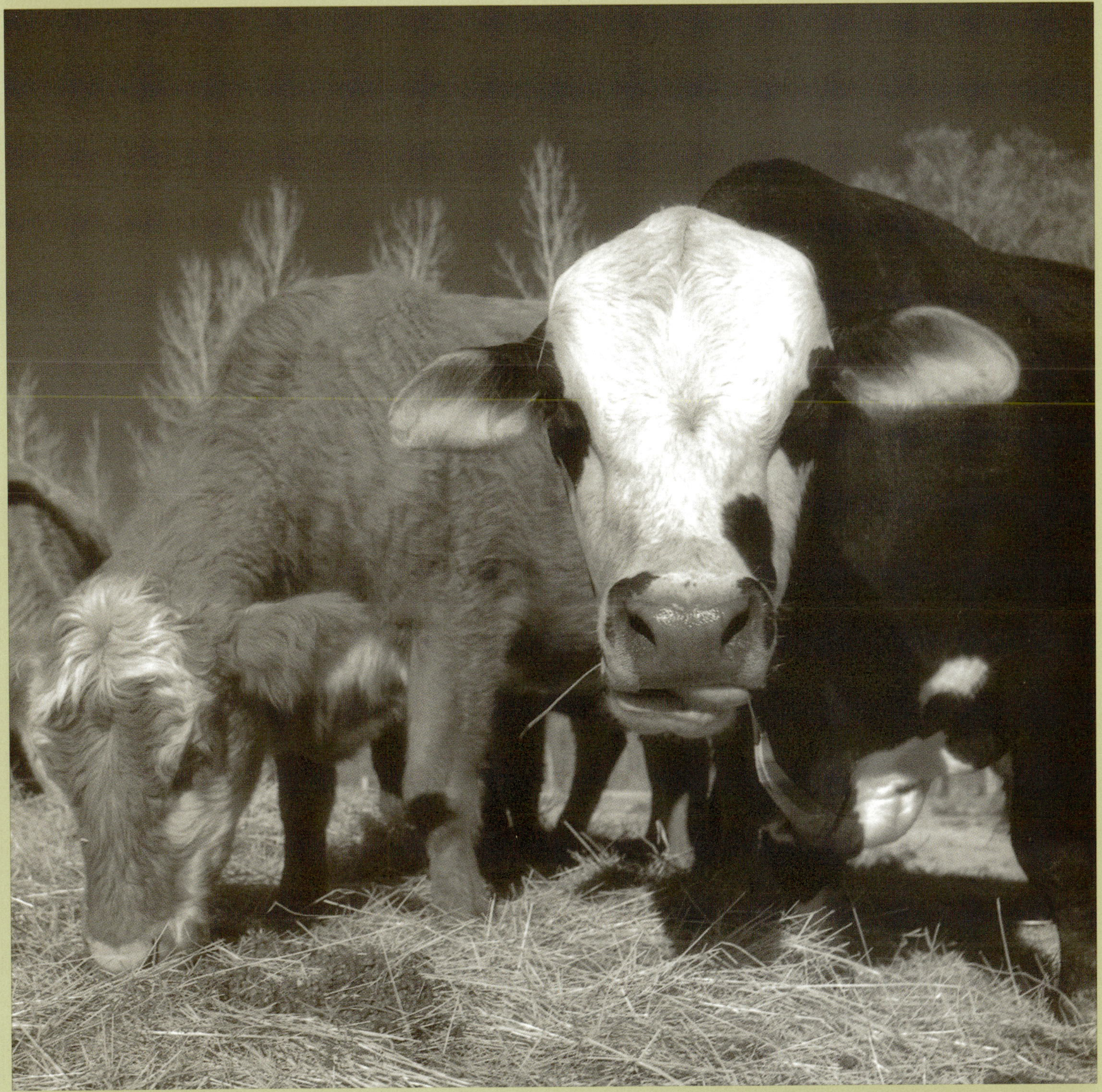

The Generosity of Cows

by Dave Prosser

Milk Don't Come From a Bottle

Milk don't come from a bottle
Milk don't come from a can
If you don't know how to milk a cow
It's time you understand
You pull and squeeze, be gentle please
And let the fun begin
Milk don't come from a bottle
Milk don't come from a can

Now Bessie is a gentle soul
And she leads a gentle life
She spends her day eating grass and hay
And chews her cud all night
She lets me milk her twice a day
But I still don't understand
She really doesn't give a thing
I have to take it all by hand.

We all take for granted
We need milk to live
But before we get a single drop
There's something has to give
So we owe a lot to Bessie
And there's just one rule
If you ever go to milk the cow
Be sure it ain't the bull.

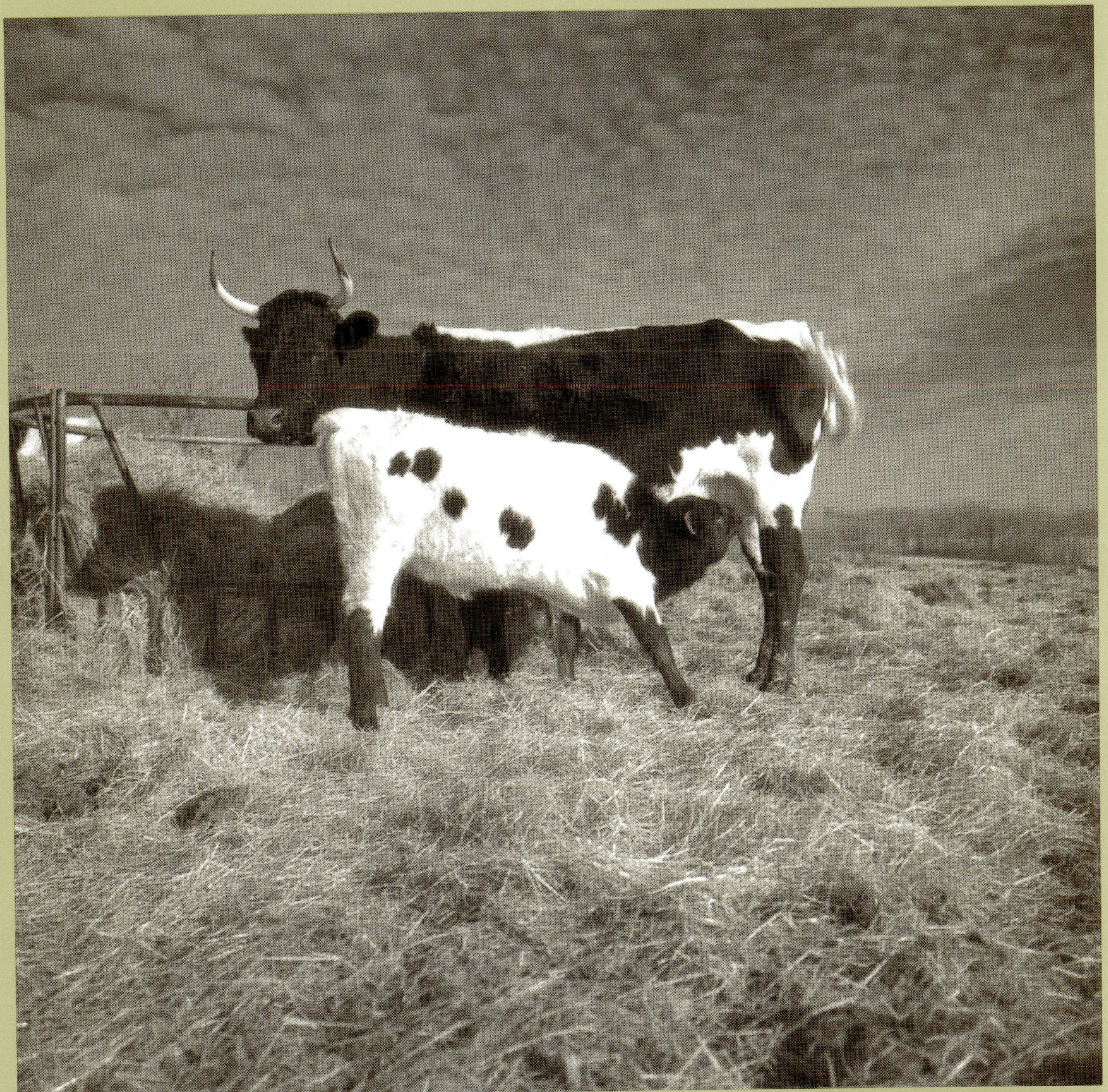

The Pornography of Cows

by Catherine Anderson

My paintings hang in collections around the world, but one of the places where they would not 'hang' was in The Lodge at Sonoma, a division of the Marriott in Sonoma County, California.

The lodge people wanted local artists to paint scenes of the area. I brought them a watercolor painting of a row of cows simply eating at their trough in a field ... a very peaceful painting. I thought they'd be honored to accept it. But someone in the hotel decided that the painting was, well, it just wasn't right; as they explained it to me, they didn't want any "provocative animal parts" hanging in the lodge! My painting was rejected.

They wanted another instead, so I brought them a watercolor entitled "Fresh Air." I thought it was a wonderful composition of cows sitting in a field, minding their business and looking peaceful. They bought this painting and gave me a check.

Soon afterward I got a call from one of the organizers who left a message on my machine. "We're having trouble with one of the cows in your painting," she said. "It's in a provocative position." At first I thought they were kidding; then I was stunned. I had never thought of my paintings as cow porn! "Which cow?" I found myself wondering. "We really want to hang your work," the message went on. "But not this one. We need to swap it for another painting."

I was not going to swap the painting. Nor did I bother to phone her back. Soon, she called again. "If you don't swap paintings," she warned, "we'll have to destroy this one!"

This was my first "censored" piece, and the story was soon reported in the *San Francisco Chronicle*. I got calls from everywhere and was interviewed by several radio stations around the country. The interviews were tough because it was hard to talk without laughing. But collectors found me again, so the press was great. The AP Wire picked up the story and it traveled around the world. Of course, the Europeans thought we Americans were nuts. In the end, the company making the prints for the entire hotel chain ended up "rescuing" and buying my painting. They said they felt "honored" to have it. So now the hotel has a bigger problem. The cows I painted are still right there in Sonoma, moseying around their pastures, naked.

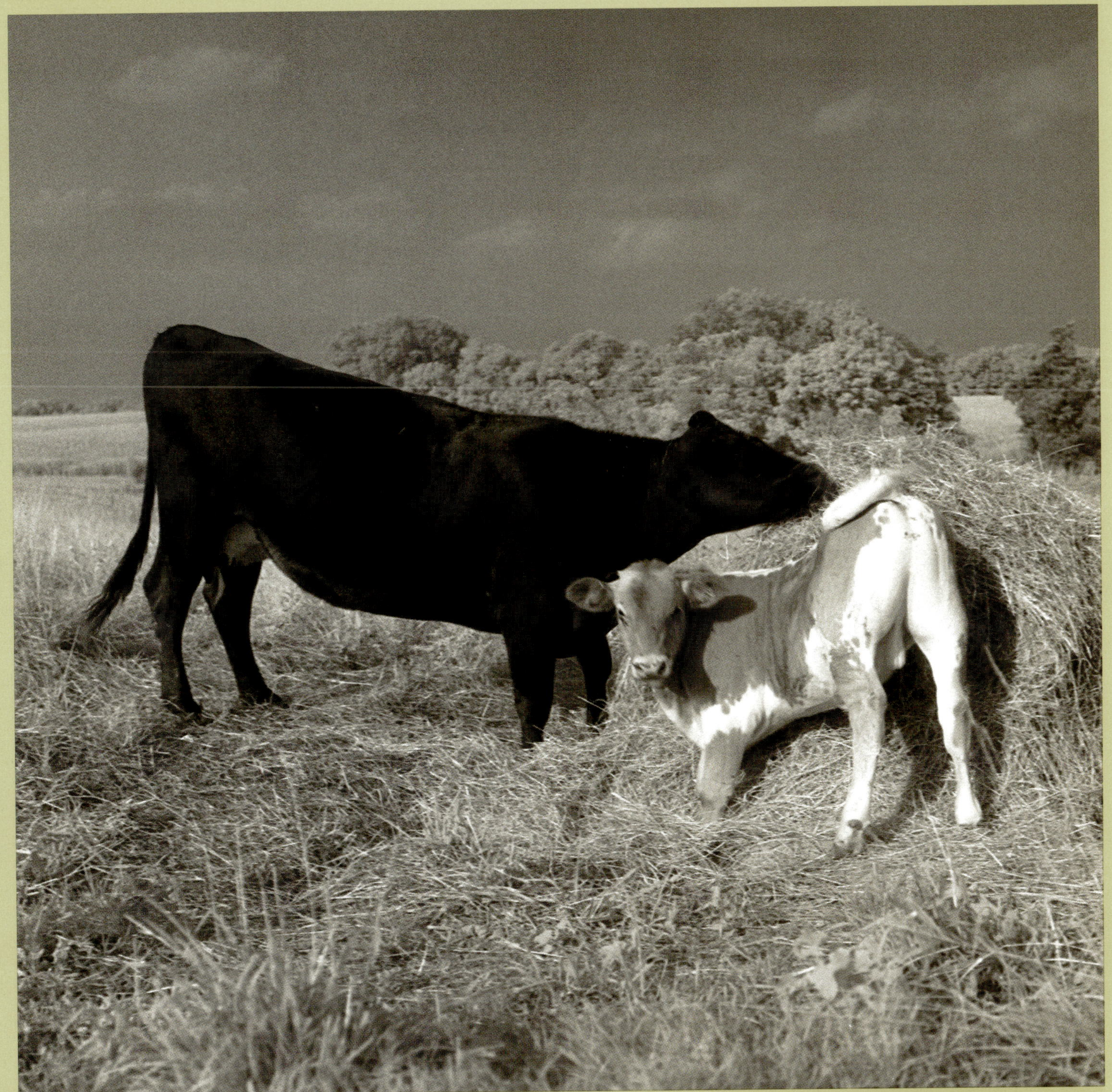

The Lesson of Cows

by Terry Kay

This is a little rhyme that I wrote for a friend, Jessie Greene, who loves cows.

A Cow Bow

There is a cow in memory,
Who had a great dislike for me.
Each time I took the milking chair
I treated her with uddermost care.
Still, she objected to every tug
As though I were a lowly thug.
She'd wait until the pail was full
Then start to act more like a bull,
Snorting and kicking all around
Until she finally knocked me down.

Yet, what I learned from all that strife
Has served me well throughout my life:
If you expect to fill your pail,
Do not be shocked if you may fail.
And milk that's spilled is milk that's gone,
And nothing leaves you more alone,
Feeling battered, beaten and sore,
Than having had, but have no more.
The answer is a simple thing:
Fill up the bucket once again.

And so I make this wordy bow
To an old and quarrelsome cow.
If she had been more friend than foe,
I would not know the things I know.

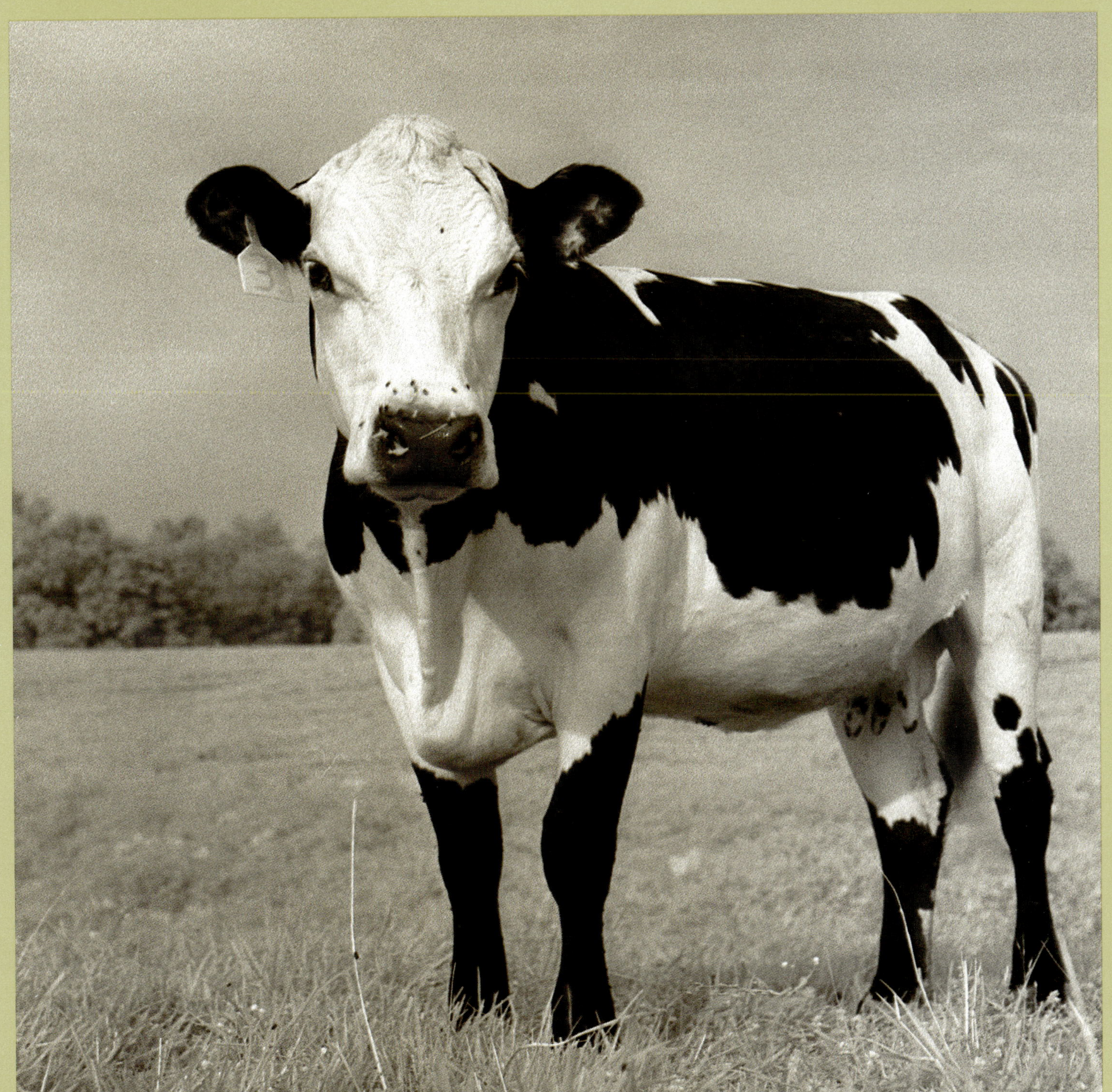

In Memorium: for Rosie

by Carl Hileman

Since I first started photographing cows, back in the summer of 1999, I have visited many farms and seen hundreds of bovine. Most of them did what cows tend to do: they grazed, mooed, and stared at me with that special cow curiosity. When I would get into position to photograph them, often lying flat on my stomach, I did my best not to disturb them. At least, that's what I told myself. In truth, I love animals, and I didn't want to get attached to any of these cows. I knew the inevitability that lies ahead for farm cattle. But, despite that, and long after I was done with the photographing, I'd find myself occasionally calling up the owners, even visiting the farms again, just to see how things were going.

"Do you still have Betsy?" I might ask. Or "Is Snowball still in the pasture?"

If the reply was "no," the conversation ended there. That's the way we dealt with it.

In the summer of 2004, while I was working on this book, I came across this photograph of Rosie. It's the one you see opposite this page. Rosie was a speckled-nosed White Face with a hairdo like a punk rocker. She had a personality all her own. She was one of those cows that would see me in the pasture and come close to check on what I was doing. Then, she'd stand there, staring at me, as if she wanted to ask about my camera, or what I was doing in *her* pasture. When I pulled this photo to put in the book, I decided to call the owner and ask about Rosie.

I made that call with the usual reservation, knowing it might be the short conversation again, and that Rosie had been "shipped." Lisa answered the phone. She and Mark, good friends for many years, maintain a small herd. I had photographed their cows many times.

"I'm just calling to see how things are going," I said. "How many cows do you have right now, and how many calves were born this spring?" Lisa gave me the rundown. And then I simply had to ask. "Is Rosie still around?" There was that long, uncomfortable pause.

"Rosie died this spring," Lisa said. "Having her calf. They both died. We didn't know until we found her." I could hear the sadness in her voice, thick and heavy. And I could hear the guilt there, too. I knew their farm well, knew how their herd could range over many acres of woodland separated by pastures. It was impossible to watch every cow, every minute of the day. And if one was having birthing trouble, the owner wouldn't always know. It wasn't anyone's fault. This was one of those accidents of nature, and it's not always easy for us to understand.

When I hung up the phone, I sat there thinking about Rosie, about how my interest in cows had begun that frosty autumn day, when I was still a teenaged boy, that morning I had helped Donny Wilkerson deliver a calf that would have otherwise died. I had blown into the two small nostrils and had seen the miracle of life stirring in those eyes. I wish I had been there to help Rosie and her calf. We are all vulnerable to nature, humans and animals alike. But unlike humans, nature gives and takes without consideration, and without dispensing special privileges. Nature is indifferent. And that cycle? It just keeps going.

This page is for Rosie.

Carl Hileman

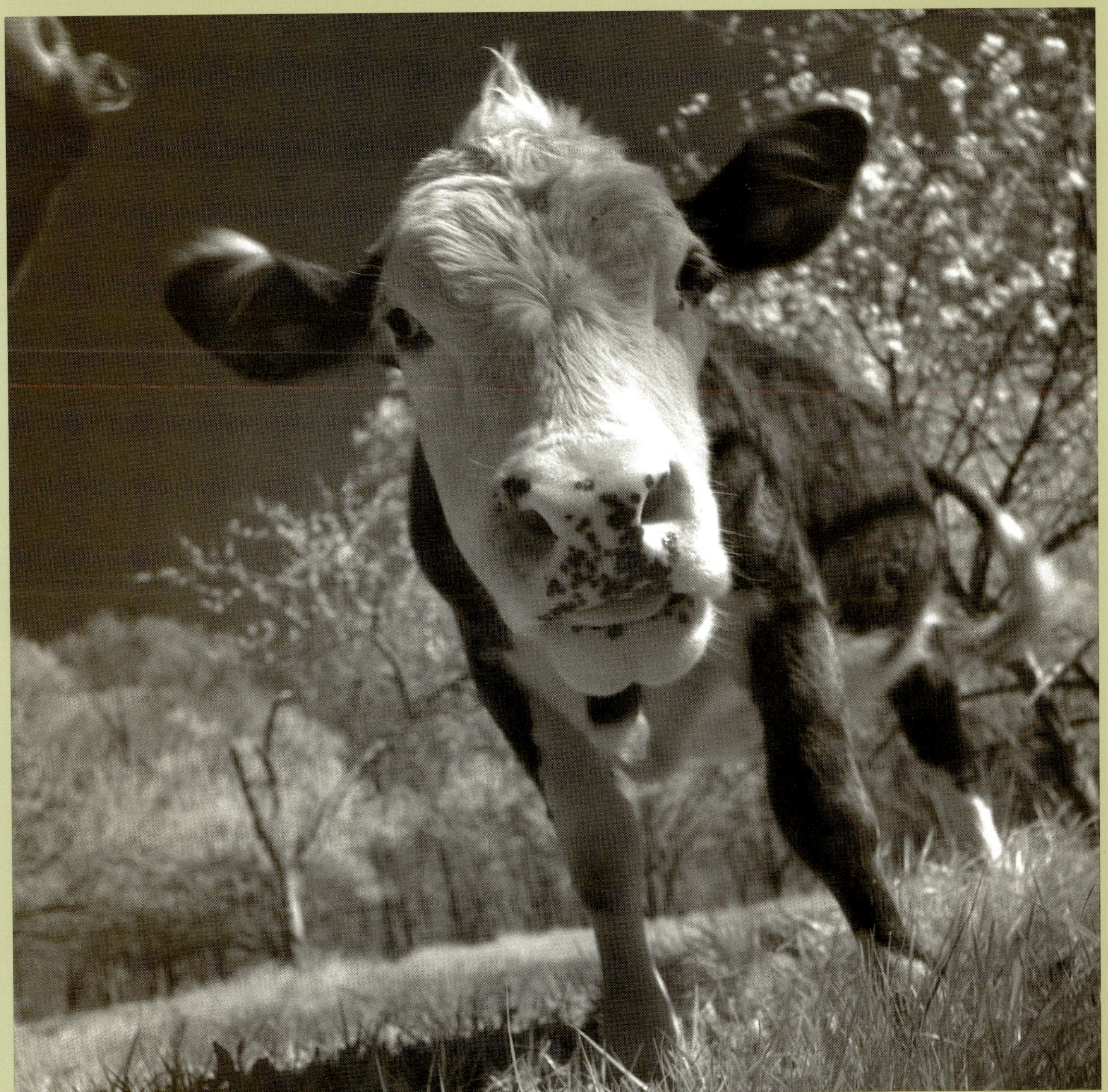

Contributors

BILL ANDERSON is one of the most awarded songwriters in the history of country music, a million-selling recording artist, TV game show host, network soap opera star, spokesman for a nationwide restaurant chain, and a performer known around the world for his classic song "Still." His songs have been recorded by Ray Price, Porter Wagoner, Debbie Reynolds, Ivory Joe Hunter, Kitty Wells, Faron Young, Lawrence Welk, Dean Martin, Jerry Lee Lewis, Aretha Franklin, Walter Brennan, and many more. A member of the Grand Ole Opry since 1961, Bill has been voted Songwriter of the Year six times, as well as Male Vocalist of the Year. He is a member of the Nashville Songwriters Hall of Fame, and the Country Music Hall of Fame. His autobiography, *Whisperin' Bill*, was published by Longstreet Press in 1989. His second book (a humorous look at the music business) *I Hope You're Living as High on the Hog as the Pig You Turned Out to Be* is in its third printing. (www.billanderson.com)

CATHERINE ANDERSON was born in Chicago and attended the American Academy of Fine Art, the University of Cincinnati, and the Academy of Art College in San Francisco. She has received numerous awards from top art organizations in the United States and teaches workshops around the world as well as one-week retreats in her Studio in the Heights in Houston. Two of her paintings appear in the movie *Dark Water*. She is the author of the *Basic Watercolor Answer Book* and has just completed her first video, *Creating Multiple Glazes in Your Watercolors.* Catherine's paintings have been exhibited in museums throughout the United States and China, are in corporate collections, and in the private collections of Will and Margaret Hearst, Patti and Gavin MacLeod, and Steven Spielberg, among others. (www.catherineanderson.net)

BILL BROWN is the author of four collections of poetry: *Holding on By Letting Go, What the Night Told Me, The Art of Dying,* and *The Gods of Little Pleasures,* and a writing text, *Important Words.* He directed the writing program at Hume-Fogg Academic Magnet School in Nashville until he retired in 2003 and accepted a part-time position at Peabody College of Vanderbilt University. He was named Distinguished Teacher in the Arts by the National Foundation for Advancement in the Arts and has been a Scholar in Poetry at the Bread Loaf Writers Conference, a Fellow at the Virginia Center for the Creative Arts, and a two-time recipient of Fellowships in Poetry from the Tennessee Arts Commission. Brown lives with his wife, Suzanne, and their cat, Soliloquy, in the hills of Robertson County, Tennessee.

JEFF BYERS has a Masters Degree in Psychology. Before he joined the Dairy Council of California, he worked as a horse patrolman for the National Park Service in Yosemite National Park. (Dairy Council of California: www.dairycouncilofca.org.)

JEFFREY A. CARVER is the author of fourteen science fiction novels, most recently *Eternity's End*, which was nominated for the Nebula Award. His *Writing Science Fiction and Fantasy* was a distance-learning television show for young aspiring writers, then a home-study course on CD-ROM, and finally an online course. A native of Ohio, he now lives outside Boston wi his wife and daughters. You can read some of his shorter work and learn more about his books at www.starrigger.net.

PATSI BALE COX has written many celebrity books, including *Nickel Dreams,* with Tanya Tucker, *Still Woman Enough* with Loretta Lynn, Jenny Jones's *My Life,* Tony Orlando's *Halfway to Paradise,* and Ralph Emery's *The Viei from Nashville* and *Fifty Years down a Country Road.* (Two memoirs she coauthored appeared on the *New York Times* Bestseller List, and one the *NY Times* Business Bestseller List.) She is coauthor of *A Country Music Christmas*, and is currently working with Wynonna Judd on a memoir. Her magazine cover story subjects include Garth Brooks, Waylon Jennings, Tammy Wynette, Willie Nelson, and Hank Williams Jr., and she has done extensive publicity work for Tanya Tucker and Garth Brooks. In the 1970s, Patsi founded one of th nation's first feminist magazines, *Colorado Woman,* and remained as editor until 1980. She served three terms on the Grammy nominating committe in the liner note category.

AUGUST WILLIAM DERLETH (1909-1971) was one of Wisconsin's mo prolific writers. His regional sagas detailing his beloved "Sac Prairie" are some of his finest works, among them *Walden West* and *Return to Walden West*. H also wrote mysteries, detective stories, horror/fantasy, historical novels, as well as poetry, and was an editor for many collections of fiction and poetry He cofounded Arkham House Publishers in 1939, with Donald Wandrei, to publish the works of Howard Philip Lovecraft. To this day, Arkham House remains the keeper of the Lovecraft legacy and is still publishing ne books. Derleth's posthumous third volume in the Sac Prairie saga, *Annals of Walden West,* is scheduled for publication in late 2004 by University Press of Madison, Wisconsin.

ELEN DOENZ lives in Lethbridge, Alberta, Canada.

EEPY JOHN ESTES was born on January 25, 1904, in Ripley, nnessee, one of a sharecropping family of ten. At age six, he was blinded his right eye from a baseball accident. Due to a chronic blood pressure order that gave him fits of narcolepsy, he was nicknamed "Sleepy John." egendary pioneer of folk-blues, Sleepy John died on June 5, 1977, d is buried in Durhamville, Tennessee. His "Milk Cow Blues" has been corded in various versions by Elvis, Aerosmith, Mark Knopfler, the nks, Bob Dylan, and many others.

ORA STRONG FARMER was born in Annville, Kentucky, on cember 16, 1902. She completed, with honors, the ten grades of school at were available in her town at the time, and went on to finish school at aryville College, near Knoxville, Tennessee. There she met her future sband, Moss Farmer, who was also from Kentucky, only ten miles from ere Flora was born. "Ten miles was a long ride by horseback in 1915," ora liked to mention. "So we never met until we went to school in nnessee." Flora and her husband had four children. An intelligent and ing woman to those who knew her, Flora told the story of her life to her n Frank Farmer, who made dozens of audio tapes, transcribed them, d had them bound. The memoir was titled *Laughter and Tears*. The story of bert Pleas and the cow is taken from that memoir. Flora Strong Farmer ed in Tampa, Florida, at the age of ninety-seven.

HARLES FISHMAN is director of the Distinguished Speakers Program at rmingdale State University and associate editor of *The Drunken Boat*. His books poetry include *Mortal Companions*, *The Firewalkers*, and *The Death Mazurka*, selected the American Library Association as one of the outstanding books of the ar. Fishman's chapbook, *Time Travel Reports*, was published by Timberline ess. His sixth book-length collection, *Chopin's Piano*, will be published by me Being Books in late 2005 or early 2006. *(www.thedrunkenboat.com)*

UL M. GAHLINGER, M.D., Ph.D., M.P.H., FACOEM is the author *Illegal Drugs: A Complete Guide to Their History, Chemistry, Use and Abuse*, forthcoming om Viking. He is currently an Adjunct Professor in the Faculty of edicine, University of Utah, Salt Lake City. His research has taken him over ninety countries, from the Arctic to Antarctica, and consulting for NASA at the Kennedy Space Center. A certified substance-abuse Medical Review Officer and Senior FAA Aviation Medical Examiner, he has studied the effect of drugs in various work settings and in the space program. He is board certified in Occupational and Environmental Medicine, and a commercial aircraft pilot with instrument and multi-engine ratings.

LARRY GATLIN From his recording debut in 1973 with "Sweet Becky Walker," to his Grammy Award-winning "Broken Lady," to the smash-hit "All the Gold in California," Larry Gatlin has proven his ability to craft songs that are loved by millions. His songs have found their way into *Billboard's* Top Five fifteen times. Many other artists have recorded Gatlin's songs, including Elvis, Barbra Streisand, Johnny Cash, Dottie West, and Johnny Mathis. Larry also appeared on the Broadway stage in 1993 for a seven-month run in the title role of the Tony-awarded musical, *The Will Rogers Follies*. He returned to the theatrical stage in 2000 and 2001 as the star of the touring company of Frank Wildhorn's Broadway musical *The Civil War*. Gatlin was recently named the Director of Artists and Performances for The Gospel Music Channel. (www.GatlinBrothers.com)

LAURA GILPIN is a poet and a nurse. She is the author of *The Hocus Pocus of the Universe*, which won the Walt Whitman Award in 1976. She also received a fellowship from the National Endowment for the Arts. After teaching writing at the Henry Street Settlement and the New York Public Library, she became a registered nurse, working in pediatrics at Memorial Sloan Kettering Cancer Hospital in New York and adult oncology and medicine at California Pacific Medical Center in San Francisco. For the past twenty years she has worked for Planetree, a non-profit organization working to humanize hospitals. She is coeditor of *Putting Patients First: Designing and Practicing Patient-Centered Care*, which received the 2004 Hamilton Book of the Year Award. She lives in Fairhope, Alabama, and is completing her second book of poetry.

JIM GLASER and his brothers, Tompall and Chuck, were members of the Grand Ole Opry for fifteen years, and not only paved the way for modern country groups, they won virtually every group award in the country music industry. Jim's solo career took off in 1980 and his first release, "When You're Not a Lady," still holds the record for being the most successful first release of a new label, staying on the national charts for thirty-four weeks.

(The album itself, *Man in the Mirror,* stayed in Billboard's charts for over a year and a half.) A follow-up release from the same album, "You're Gettin' to Me Again," went to number one. His newest CD, released in 2004, is *Me and My Dream*. Of the many songs Glaser has written, his most successful to date is "Woman, Woman," first recorded by Gary Puckett & the Union Gap (later by Glaser himself on his *Man in the Mirror* CD) and now a pop classic. (www.jimglaser.com)

RICK HAUTALA has had more than twenty books published, including the million-copy, international bestseller *Nightstone* as well as *Twilight Time, Little Brothers, Beyond the Shroud, Cold Whisper,* and *Impulse*, and more than sixty short stories that have appeared in a variety of national and international anthologies and magazines. With Bill Relling, he has written six screenplays. Rick's most recently published books include two *Body of Evidence* books written with Christopher Golden: *Last Breath* and *Throat Culture* (Pocket); a paperback edition of his C.D. Publications hardcover *Bedbugs* (Leisure); and a novel under the pseudonym A. J. Matthews, titled *Looking Glass* (Berkley). A graduate of the University of Maine in Orono with a Master of Arts in English Literature, Rick lives in southern Maine with author Holly Newstein. (www.rickhautala.com)

ERICA JOHNSON lives on a dairy farm operated by her family in Minnesota. She still helps milk cows morning and night. She wrote the essay in this collection when she was only eleven years old as part of a school project. She's now fifteen, and about to enter tenth grade. Erica shows dairy cattle, beef cattle, and pigs in competitions at county fairs, and sometimes the state fair. She usually wins first place. She plans to work in the dairy industry.

TERRY KAY has written many acclaimed novels—*The Year the Lights Came On, After Eli, Dark Thirty, Shadow Song, The Runaway, The Kidnapping of Aaron Greene, Taking Lottie Home, The Valley of Light*—and a collection of essays, *Special Kay: The Wisdom of Terry Kay*. But is it his novel *To Dance with the White Dog* that has taken its place among Southern literary classics. The film of the same name was presented in 1993 as a Hallmark Hall of Fame movie for CBS, starring Hume Cronyn and Jessica Tandy. The production earned the highest television rating of the season, with more than thirty-three million viewers, and Cronyn won that year's Emmy for Best Actor, in the role of Sam Peek, the character based on Kay's father. Terry Kay is also the author of the children's book *To Whom the Angel Spoke: A Story of the Christmas. The Runaway* was also produced as a Hallmark Hall of Fame movie for CBS, featuring Dean Cain and Maya Angelou. (www.terrykay.com)

DOUG KERSHAW, fiddler extraordinaire, singer, and songwriter, is considered the first Cajun superstar. His classic song "Louisiana Man," which tells of his early days on a houseboat with Mama Rita and Daddy Jack, was the first song broadcast back from outer space. A consummate performer, Kershaw still tours the world with his band, appearing at major music festivals, such as the New Orleans Jazz Festival. He also has performed during halftime at the Superbowl. He is currently signed to perform 143 days a year at a musical theater in Branson, Missouri. His latest CD, *Two-Step Fever*, is a collection of Cajun French houseboat songs. (www.dougkershaw.com)

MIKE KIMBALL is the author of the comic novel *Firewater Pond* and three suspense novels, all set in Maine: *Green Girls, Mouth to Mouth*, and the bestselling *Undone*, which received the Fresh Talent Award in the U.K. and is still published worldwide. He has written two stage plays and several screenplays and adaptations for motion picture companies, as well as episodes for the TV show *Monsters*. His latest screenplay, *Trap Line*, is an adaptation of a novel in progress.

SUE McCLURE is a staff writer for the *Tennessean* newspaper in Nashville. She has also worked for the *Memphis Commercial-Appeal,* the *Columbia Daily Heral[d]* the *Franklin Review-Appeal* and the now defunct *Nashville Banner*.

WESLEY McNAIR is the author of seven collections of poetry and editor [of] two anthologies of contemporary writing. He is the recipient of fellowship[s] from the Rockefeller, Fulbright, and Guggenheim Foundations, several National Endowments for the Arts, and numerous awards, including the Robert Frost Prize, the Devins Award for poetry, and the Theodore Roeth[ke] prize. He served on the Nominating Jury for the Pulitzer Prize in poetry f[or] 2002. He wrote the script for a PBS-aired series on Robert Frost, for whi[ch] he received an Emmy Award. Featured on Garrison Keillor's *Writer's Almana[c]* and NPR's *Weekend Edition,* his work has appeared in the *Pushcart Prize Annual, Th[e] Best American Poetry,* and over fifty anthologies and textbooks.

[MI]CHAEL McNEILLY spent seventeen years in Hollywood, facing up to [sca]ry things. He was a resident member of the Mark Taper Forum's Acting [En]semble in Los Angeles and has acted in over fifty productions, ranging [fro]m the Taper to the Kennedy Center in Washington, D.C. He has served [as] Guest Artist in Theater at numerous universities, and has guest-starred [on] television in *MacGyver, Knot's Landing,* and *The Tortellis,* to name a few. And he [wa]s also a Mighty Carson Art Player on the *Tonight Show* with Johnny Carson. [He] currently resides in Helena, Montana, where he is the director of [Ti]meprov, a theater company which is currently touring his production of *[Th]e Lost Journals of Lewis and Clark,* and where cows are known as "slow elk."

[C]ATHERINE "KATE" O'LEARY and her husband, Patrick, lived in [a c]ottage at 137 DeKoven Street, on Chicago's West Side. At 9 P.M. on [Su]nday night, October 8, 1871, a fire started in or near the cow barn [be]hind their cottage. It soon jumped the river's south branch and by [1:]30 A.M. the entire business district was in flames. It then raced [no]rthward across the main river. By the time the fire was out, three [hu]ndred were dead, 100,000 homeless, and 18,000 buildings were [re]duced to ashes. The property loss was estimated at over $200 million. [Ru]mor spread that Mrs. O'Leary had told neighbors that her cow had [kic]ked over a lantern in the barn. This is not factual, and yet the myth grew [fas]ter than the fire spread. And it remains to this day.

[K]ATHIE PELLETIER is the author of six novels under her own [na]me, which include *The Funeral Makers, Beaming Sonny Home,* and *The Weight of [Wa]ter,* which won the New England Book Award for Fiction. Under the [pse]udonym of K.C. McKinnon she has written two novels, *Dancing at the [Har]vest Moon,* which was translated to nineteen languages, and was a CBS TV [fil]m, starring Jacqueline Bisset and Valerie Harper, and *Candles on Bay Street,* [wh]ich was translated to ten languages. She has written a screenplay, based [on] *The Funeral Makers,* to be directed by Doug Liman. Pelletier has had songs [rec]orded by the Glaser Brothers, the Texas Tornados, and David Bryne. [(ww]w.kcmckinnon.com)

[H]IS DIVINE GRACE A.C. BHAKTIVEDNATA SWAMI [P]RABHUPADA was born in 1896 in Calcutta, India. He first met his [spi]ritual master, Srila Bhaktisiddhanta Sarasvati Gosvami, in Calcutta [in] 1922. In just twelve years, despite his advanced age, Srila Prabhupada circled the globe fourteen times on lecture tours that took him to six continents. Yet this vigorous schedule did not slow his prolific literary output. His writings constitute a veritable library of Vedic philosophy, religion, literature, and culture.

DAVE "Doc" PROSSER was born and grew up in the hills of Southern Illinois. Raised up in an "old time" music and bluegrass environment, Dave began writing, singing, and playing music at the age of fifteen. He is currently the lead singer and banjo player for the group *Old Santa Fe,* whose first CD was *Music of the Hills*. The band has just finished their second CD, *Iron Mountain Line*. Along with his musical talent, Dave has appeared in two historical documentaries which aired on the History Channel, *Pirates of Cave in Rock,* and *Frontier Doctors*. He currently lives in the hills with his wife, Glenda, overlooking the Mississippi River, not far from where the Ohio and Mississippi meet.

DAVE PROWSE is a world-renowned weightlifter and body builder. He trained such celebrities as Christopher Reeve, for his role in *Superman.* An actor, he has appeared in many films, including Stanley Kubrick's *A Clockwork Orange.* It is his role as Darth Vader, in George Lucas's first three *Star Wars* films (all five *Star Wars* films are ranked in theTop 25 All-Time Highest Grossing Movies) that has turned him into a world-wide icon among the legions of loyal fans. He is at work on his memoir, *Behind the Mask.* (www.darthvader.com)

SANDY RICHARDSON is the author of *The Girl Who Ate Chicken Feet*, which was published by Dial Books for Young Readers in 1998, received an outstanding merit rating in Bank Street College's *The Best Children's Books of the Year*, 1999, and was nominated for the South Carolina Junior Book Award in 2001-2002. She is also an editor and contributing columnist for *Imagine That!*, a monthly magazine for children, parents, and teachers. Harcourt Brace contracted with her to edit and write for the fiction section of its *Instructor's Resource Guide to Literature: Reading*Reacting*Writing*.

GEORGE RODRIGUE's pop culture icon BLUE DOG (used by Xerox and Absolut Vodka) is now famous around the world. His large following of devoted fans who acquire his Blue Dog paintings include Hillary Rodham Clinton, Whoopi Goldberg, Tom Brokaw, and many other celebrity collectors. His art has been published in five books, including *Blue Dog Man,* which has a foreword by Tom Brokaw. His most recent book is *The Art of George Rodrigue*, with a text by art historian and former ART news correspondent Ginger Danto, and a preface by Michael Lewis. He has two art galleries, one in New Iberia, L.A., and one in Carmel, CA. (www.georgerodrigue.com)

JACK SAGE was a colorful historian and writer from Tacoma, Washington, who was known for his popular local tales of ghosts and other events. Jack passed away in 1996. His wife, Dawn Sage, granted permission to use this story in Jack's memory.

SHIRLEY SKEEL is a freelance print and radio journalist who has lived in the United States, Canada, England, and Australia. She has worked for major newspapers and magazines, writing business, travel, and human interest stories. She is exceptionally fond of Jersey cows, but has disliked milk since childhood.

VERNON L. SMITH is the co-winner of the 2003 Nobel Prize for Economics, and the author or co-author of more than two hundred books and articles on the subjects of finance, natural resource economics, capital theory, and experimental economics. Smith holds a bachelor's degree in Electrical Engineering from Cal Tech and a Ph.D. in Economics from Harvard. He currently serves as Professor of Economics and Law at George Mason University. In addition, he is a research scholar in the Interdisciplinary Center for Economic Science and is a Fellow of the Mercatus Center in Arlington, Virginia. His papers in Experimental Economics were published by The Cambridge University Press in 1991, followed by a second collection of his recent work in Bargaining and Market Behavior in 2000.

PAUL SYLBERT is a film Production Designer who won an Oscar for *Heaven Can Wait,* starring Warren Beatty. The titles of some of Sylbert's many other films include *Kramer Vs. Kramer; One Flew Over the Cuckoo's Nest; The Pope of Greenwich Village; Gorky Park; Prince of Tides* (for which he was nominated for an Oscar), *Biloxi Blues; Rosewood; Free Willy 2; Sliver; Blow Out; Conspiracy Theory; Fresh Horses, Mikey and Nicky; Ishtar; The Grass Harp; Hardcore*; and *Wolfen.* He was Art Director for Elia Kazan's *Face in the Crowd,* and Alfred Hitchcock's *The Wrong Man*. As a director, Sylbert directed Richard Benjamin in *The Steagle,* and is the author of the book *Final Cut: The Making and Breaking of a Film,* and the screenplay *Night Hawks,* starring Sylvester Stallone.

TANYA TUCKER is a performer and recording artist whose celebrity status has one of the highest television "Q" factors of all country stars. He recording catalogue includes more than one hundred solo and compilatic albums. Ms. Tucker achieved international fame at the age of thirteen when her single "Delta Dawn" soared to the top of the charts, winning he first Grammy nomination at the age of fifteen. She has been honored wit the highest awards country music can offer and has recorded too many Top Ten and Number One songs to count. She was named one of the Top Ten Female Country Artists of all time by *Radio and Records* and was the first female country music artist to appear on the cover of *Rolling Stone.* He autobiography, *Nickel Dreams,* was a *New York Times* bestseller.

IAN TYSON is one of a kind in the world of music. Spanning three decades, Tyson has forged a trail of musical innovation, starting with the legendary folk duo of Ian and Sylvia in the 1960s, and culminating with t seminal *Cowboyography* collection, reaching platinum status in the mid 199 Author, singer, and songwriter, Tyson has written many hits, including t classic "Four Strong Winds." He lives on his ranch in the Rocky Mountai of Alberta, Canada. (www.iantyson.com)

SANDRA ADELMUND WITT first published her poetry while an undergraduate at the University of Northern Iowa. That small volume, entitled *Bringing Up Baby,* was the predecessor to work at the University of Iowa Writer's Workshop, and an MFA in poetry from the University of Montana. Sandra won the Minnesota Voices Project competition in 199 and subsequently published *Aerial Studies.* She has published numerous poe in literary journals and magazines, and continues to write in her spare ti She is working on a Master's Degree in Special Education, and now works with Special Ed children.